Jensen's Grammar

Your One Stop Source for Learning Grammar

Text & Exercises
by
Frode Jensen

Dedicated to all my former students who graciously endured working
through these exercises in their many trial forms,
to those teachers, parents, and children who have chosen to stand against
the tide and make a difference in education,
and to those great folks who in the beginning encouraged me to get
my books finished and brought into print.

2010 edition

ISBN 978-1-886061-38-5

Jensen's Grammar

Table of Contents

To the Students Using this Book   4

CHARTS

Chart 1	Form Words Chart	5
Chart 2	Function Words Chart	6
Chart 3	Basic Sentence Patterns Sheet	7
Chart 4	Keys to Formula Writing	8
Chart 5	Verbals and Major Punctuation	9

LESSONS

Lesson 1	Basic Sentences	10
Lesson 2	Nouns as Namers	12
Lesson 3	Noun Plurals	14
Lesson 4	Nouns: Possession	16
Lesson 5	Nouns: Derivational Suffixes	18
Lesson 6	Noun Functions 1	20
Lesson 7	Noun Markers	22
Lesson 8	Test Frames	24
Lesson 9	Pronouns	26
Lesson 10	Prepositions	28
Lesson 11	Verb Types	30
Lesson 12	Verb Forms	32
Lesson 13	Auxiliary Verbs	34
Lesson 14	Verb Cluster Syntax	36
Lesson 15	Verbs: Derivational Suffixes	38
Lesson 16	Transitive & Intransitive Verbs	40
Lesson 17	Noun Subject & Verb Agreement	42
Lesson 18	Case in Pronominal Nouns	44
Lesson 19	Adjectives: Function & Position	46
Lesson 20	Adjectives: Forms of Degree	48
Lesson 21	Adjectives: Derivational Suffixes	50
Lesson 22	Adverbs	52
Lesson 23	Intensifiers	54
Lesson 24	Formula Writing	56
Lesson 25	Internal Punctuation 1	58
Lesson 26	Noun Functions 2	60
Lesson 27	Noun Functions 3	62
Lesson 28	Noun Functions 4	64
Lesson 29	Looking to the Left	66
Lesson 30	Adjective Subject Complement	68
Lesson 31	Basic Sentence Patterns	70
Lesson 32	Prepositional Phrase Placement	72
Lesson 33	Noun Cluster Syntax	74
Lesson 34	Internal Punctuation 2	76

Lesson 35	Usage: *Lie/Lay, Sit/Set, Rise/Raise*	78
Lesson 36	Appositives	80
Lesson 37	Compound Pronoun Usage	82
Lesson 38	Transformations 1: *Yes/No, There* Types	84
Lesson 39	Transformations 2: Passives	86
Lesson 40	Major Punctuation 1: I, c/c I.	88
Lesson 41	Major Punctuation 2: I sub I.	90
Lesson 42	Major Punctuation 3: Sub I, I.	92
Lesson 43	Major Punctuation 4: I; I.	94
Lesson 44	Major Punctuation 5: I; c/a, I. *et. al.*	96
Lesson 45	Major Punctuation 6: Combinations	98
Lesson 46	Relative Patterns 1: Introduction	100
Lesson 47	Relative Patterns 2: *Who & Whom*	102
Lesson 48	Relative Patterns 3: Punctuation	104
Lesson 49	Relative Patterns 4: OP Variations	106
Lesson 50	Relative Patterns 5: S LV N Variations	108
Lesson 51	Relative Patterns 6: From Passives	110
Lesson 52	Relative Patterns 7: Combinations	112
Lesson 53	Noun Functions 5: Review	114
Lesson 54	Infinitives 1	116
Lesson 55	Infinitives 2: Function - Modifier	118
Lesson 56	Infinitives 3: Function - Noun Subs	120
Lesson 57	Infinitives 4: Compounds & Inserts	122
Lesson 58	Infinitives 5: Summation	124
Lesson 59	Gerunds 1: Form & Function	126
Lesson 60	Gerunds 2: Subject Complements	128
Lesson 61	Gerunds 3: Phrases	130
Lesson 62	Gerunds 4: Compounds & Inserts	132
Lesson 63	Gerunds 5: Summation	134
Lesson 64	Participles 1: Definition & Function	136
Lesson 65	Participles 2: *-EN* Forms	138
Lesson 66	Participles 3: Punctuation & Placement	140
Lesson 67	Participles 4: Generation	142
Lesson 68	Participles 5: Compounds & Inserts	144
Lesson 69	Participles 6: Summation	146
Lesson 70	Verbal Differences	148
Lesson 71	Verbal Notes	150
Lesson 72	Parallelism	152
Lesson 73	Internal Punctuation 3: Modifiers	154
Lesson 74	Noun & Verb Functions: Review	156
Lesson 75	Structural Alternatives	158

OTHER

Additional Exercises	161-189
Index of Grammatical Terms	191-194

To the Students Using this Book

Dear Student:

The rationale for this book is to teach grammar as a means, not an end. The idea is for you, the student, to practice writing the various constructions in a correct manner so that familiarity with such constructions will be achieved. After familiarity follows use; in other words, after you master the relative clause or the infinitive phrase, you will naturally utilize such constructions in writing. No one uses unfamiliar tools with ease; it only comes with practice. Writing your own sentences to satisfy the formulas found at the end of most exercises will give you that practice.

The lessons and exercises were built with three concepts in mind. First, spaced repetition is the key to learning; hence, there is constant review in every lesson. This concept is found in many good textbooks, particularly in John Saxon's math books. Second, the information is given incrementally; that is, the material comes in a natural progression of detail and concept interwoven so as to move you along with something new each lesson while fitting it in with the material previously learned and practiced. Third, the sentences in the exercises will generally set a scene or describe an action. Thus, they are usually more interesting reading in themselves instead of the random sentences in exercises found in most grammar texts. Hopefully you will enjoy the little scenarios; I think it makes the lessons much more palatable. In fact, some students have continued or expanded on the scenarios when writing their own sentences on the formula writing section of the exercises.

To get multiple uses from the text and make it easier to grade the assignments, you should put your answers on a separate sheet of paper instead of writing in the textbook itself. There really isn't adequate room on some of the exercises to fit your answers, particularly when you are called upon to write your own sentences to comply with the formulas.

As author and publisher, I grant the right to photocopy the charts for personal use. In fact, I encourage it. You or your teacher should photocopy the charts, especially the first two. Copy them onto colored paper and encase them in plastic; you should refer to them on every lesson and even on tests. Having them copied will make them readily accessible instead of having to flip back and forth in your book to use them. Learn to use those charts. They have all the essential information from which you can derive many answers. Of course, in the process you will learn much grammar as well.

This book and the others I have written are the products of over twenty-five years of experience and testing in both traditional classroom and home school settings. Others have worked through the materials independently as well. Varying degrees of success have been achieved, but everyone has been the richer for the experience. My prayer is that the same will be true for you.

Sincerely,

Frode Jensen
Author and publisher

Form Words

Word Type or Class	Miscellaneous	Function	Test Frame	Inflectional	Derivational
N Noun	it names; often marked by a NM	S - subject O - object OP - object of preposition IO - indirect object SC - subject complement MOD - modifier	(The) ____ is/are good.	Plural (E)S Possessive '(S)	-ment, -ness, -er/or, -ist -tion/sion, -ity, -ism, -hood, -dom
V Verb	**ACTIVE** shows action ------------ **LINKING (LV)** state of being both types show 2 tenses: past & present	tells what the subject is doing ------------ links the subject to the subject complement	Let's ____ (it). ------------ be, become, remain, look, appear, taste, smell, sound, feel, act, grow, **seem**	"Today I ____." *simple form* "Today he ____." *-s form* "I am ____." *-ing form* "Yesterday I ____." *-ed form* "I have ____." *-en form*	-ate -ify -ize -en
A Adjective	it limits (describes)	usually describes a noun	He/it seems ____.	DEGREE positive/simple comparative/ -er(more) superlative/ -est(most)	-ish, -ous, -ful, -less, -al, -like -able/ible
B Adverb	tells where, when, or how; moveable	usually tells about a verb			-ly

Function Words

Type/Class	Function	Test Frame	Listings
NM noun marker	marks a noun tells a noun is coming up	in _____ box(es)	**a**, **an**, **the**, my, our, your, her, his, its, their, that, these, every, each, any both, some, many, much, few, several, all, most more, either, neither
P preposition	shows a space or time relationship between two nouns	The kite flew _____ the clouds. _____ the game she slept.	usually found in a phrase with a noun (*to the store*) in, by, for, **of**, with, at, before, after, during, near, down, to, from, until
I intensifier	intensifies the meaning of adjectives & adverbs	The ___ big dog ran ____ quickly.	**very**, rather, somewhat, slightly, tremendously
M modal	helping verb which shows probability always comes before other verbs in a cluster		can, could, shall, should, will, would, may, might, must
Sub subordinating conjunction	introduces dependent clauses; shows a causal relationship I sub I Sub I, I		if, as, when, where, because, since, before, after, while, until, unless, although, though, as if, whereas, so that
c/c coordinating conjunction	connects two equal grammatical units I, c/c I		**FANBOYS** for, and, nor, but, or, yet, so
c/a conjunctive adverb	weak connector of two ideas I; c/a, I		however, nevertheless, therefore, in fact, thus, moreover, consequently, hence, furthermore
Rel relative	introduces a relative clause; shows relation (refers back) to a prior noun		who, whom, whose, which, that

NOTE: not all lists are complete; some words which occur on two different lists may be determined by substitution.

Basic Sentence Patterns Information Sheet
(Lesson 31 Supplement)

TERMINOLOGY:

S = subject   O = object   IO = indirect object
V = verb   LV = linking verb
Nsc = noun subject complement (PN)   Asc = adjective subject complement (PA)
B = adverbial constructions (includes most Pp's)
Vbw = verb base word, the main verb of the clause; it is **always the last verb** in
  a string of verbs: ☞ may have been eating   *eating* = Vbw

☞ **NOTE:** In the patterns only the Vbw is listed; helpers do not affect the pattern.

PATTERNS:

#1	S - V - (B)	One patterns quickly.
#2	S - V - O	Two has an object.
#3	S - LV - Nsc	Three is a noun.
#4	S - LV - Asc	Four seems descriptive.
#5	S - V - IO - O	Five gives the pattern another object.

PROCEDURE:

1. Find the Vbw (main verb).
2. Determine if the Vbw is **active** or **linking**.
   A. if ACTIVE verb, ask the question what? and look to the right of the Vbw.
       no answer   = pattern #1
       1st noun   = pattern #2
       2nd noun   = pattern #5
   B. if LINKING verb, try a matching form of *seem* in its place.
       if *seem* works = pattern #4
       if *seem* doesn't work, try a matching form of *equal*.
       if *equal* works = pattern #3
       if *equal* doesn't work, proceed as if the verb is active.

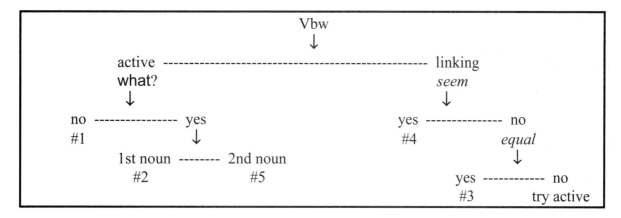

MISCELLANEOUS INFORMATION:

Pattern #1	ends in a verb or B construction	(B) constructions tell where, when, and how
Pattern #2	answers the question what?	
Pattern #3	equality pattern, S = Nsc, they name the same thing, reversible	
	be, become, & *remain* the only LV's that fit LV + NM is giveaway	
Pattern #4	*seem* or one of its forms will always fit, Asc describes the subject	
Pattern #5	two nouns follow the verb verb is a *give* type	
	can be rewritten as a Pattern #2 by putting the IO into a Pp as the OP	
☞ **NOTE:**	all modifiers (Pp's, B's, Rp's, most A's) can be dropped to determine the basic pattern	

Keys to Formula Writing

Formula writing is writing that follows a formula. Commonly the formula will utilize abbreviations for the various words or word groups to be used in the sentence. At times the abbreviation will reflect a WORD CLASS. At other times it may represent a FUNCTION such as subject or object, or it may stand for a GROUP OF WORDS such as a prepositional phrase. A list of common abbreviations and their meanings follow.

N	noun	NM	noun marker	A	adjective
V	verb (usually active)	LV	linking verb	M	modal verb
B	adverb	I	intensifier	P	preposition
Pp	prepositional phrase	S	subject (simple)	OP	object preposition
O	direct object	IO	indirect object	APPOS	appositive
Rp	relative pattern (clause)			BE	a form of *BE* as an auxiliary verb
HAVE	a form of *HAVE* as an auxiliary verb			Vbw	main verb, verb base word
Nsc/Asc	noun/adjective subject complement			Nbw	main noun, noun base word
c/c	the words *AND, OR*, and a few others			sub	subordinators: *IF, WHEN, BECAUSE...*
c/a	conjunctive adverbs: *HOWEVER, THEREFORE...*				

Here are some practical suggestions for writing a five sentence paragraph according to formulas. First, construct the basic parts of all five sentences. After the basic format is in place, you should then flesh out the sentence according to the complete formula given. Look at the example below.

1. Pp S *BE* V O Pp
2. NM A S Pp LV Asc Pp
3. S Pp Pp V I B Pp
4. S P OP c/c OP *HAVE* V O c/c O Pp
5. Pp NM A S V O P A OP

The first step is to decide on the subject to write about and then to put down the basic sentences.

1. The boys eat ice cream.	S V O
2. The ice cream is good.	S LV Asc
3. The boys talk.	S V
4. The boys eat vanilla and blackberry.	S V O & O
5. The coach paid the bill.	S V O

The final step is to fill in the extras.

1. After the game the boys are eating ice cream with their coach.
2. The fresh ice cream in their bowls is good for their egos.
3. The boys in the shade of the awning talk very excitedly about the game.
4. The boys in uniforms and hats have eaten vanilla and blackberry with much conversation.
5. In the end their fine coach paid the bill with good humor.

It is wise not to use proper names in the basic sentences since many modifiers do not fit well with them. Proper names can replace general terms after the full paragraph is written should you think it desirable to do so. The basic sentences can be altered somewhat by changing nouns when creating the finished sentence, but be careful to keep the pattern intact. Pp's that begin sentences usually make some reference to time.

Verbals

INFINITIVE: a *TO* + verb combination which either 1) substitutes for a noun, or
2) modifies some part of the sentence

GERUND: an *-ING* form of a verb which substitutes for a noun

PARTICIPLE: an *-ING* or *-EN* form of a verb used as a modifier

*A **VERBAL** is a verb which retains some qualities of a verb but does the job of an adjective
or a noun. It modifies or acts as a noun substitute. All of the above are verbals.*

TYPE	FORM	FUNCTION
infinitive	*to* + verb	modifier or noun substitute
gerund	*-ing*	noun substitute
participle	*-ing, -en*	modifier

Major Punctuation

I = Independent Clause

c/c = Coordinate Conjunction (FANBOYS)
For, And, Nor, But, Or, Yet, So

sub = Subordinators

after*	although	as	as if	because	before*	if
since	so that	till	though	unless	until*	when
	whereas	where	while	* = also prepositions		

c/a = Conjunctive Adverbs

also	besides	consequently	for example	furthermore	hence	however
instead	in addition	in fact	likewise	meanwhile	moreover	nevertheless
similarly	therefore	Thus				

Basic Rules

Rule 1:	**I, c/c I.**		Rule 4:	**I; I.**
Rule 2:	**I sub I.**		Rule 5:	**I; c/a, I.**
Rule 3:	**Sub I, I.**			**I; I, c/a.**
				I; xxx, c/a, xxx.

Lesson 1   Basic Sentences

A **basic simple sentence** generally conforms to FOUR conditions. Each condition is discussed separately below, but all four must be met in order for a group of words to be considered a basic sentence.

❶ It expresses a complete thought.

The sentence is final in itself; it does not need to go on. The thought expressed is able to stand on its own.

☞ The boy skated across the ice.
☞ The baby cried.
☞ Some of our friends from Toledo arrived yesterday after dinner.

All of the above are complete in themselves. ☞ **NOTE:** the length of the sentence does not have much to do with the completeness of thought.

❷ Two grammatical parts are present.

The **two parts** of a **basic simple sentence** are the **SUBJECT** and the **PREDICATE**.

The SUBJECT is the **naming part** of the sentence. It comes **first** and **contains** either a **noun** or a word or phrase functioning as a noun.

The PREDICATE comes **second** and is the **telling part**. It always **contains a verb**.

This book will use a double line (//) to separate the two parts. Remember that the subject is first while the predicate follows. It is a natural order since something (the subject) has to be identified so that an action or observation (the predicate) can take place.

☞ The boy // skated across the ice.
☞ Babies // cry.
☞ An old man from the center of town // fell yesterday.
☞ Eating tacos heaped with cheese // was his idea of fun.

You will note that the **predicate almost always begins with a verb** of some kind. The **subject** usually points out or **names "who"** or **"what"** while the **predicate tells** what was **done** or **observed**.

❸ A sentence begins with a capital letter.

This rule is obvious to all and only needs to be stated to be recognized. The capital letter on the first word of any sentence is simply a device for the convenience of the reader so that he will know when a new thought is beginning.

❹ A sentence ends with some type of end punctuation.

A basic simple sentence will end with a period almost all of the time. Other end punctuation marks are the **exclamation point** (!) and the **question mark** (?), but questions are not basic simple sentences, and true exclamatory sentences are relatively rare.

Basic Sentences   Exercise 1

1. List the four conditions necessary for a simple basic sentence.
2. What type of word always occurs in a predicate?
3. Where in the predicate does this type of word usually occur?
4. What is the function of a predicate in a sentence?
5. What type of word normally occurs in a subject?
6. What is the function of a subject in a sentence?
7. What is the order of occurrence for a subject and a predicate?
8. Name the common end punctuation found at the end of a basic sentence?
9. What punctuation is used at the beginning of a sentence?
10. Which basic sentence part tells who or what the sentence is talking about?
11. Which basic sentence part tells what went on or what was observed?

Label each of the following as SUBJECT or PREDICATE depending on which they could function as.

12. my friend in the other room
13. some of the men at work
14. ate a whole chicken by himself
15. was a real drag
16. had been fighting for seven years
17. will want to go home afterwards
18. four horsemen
19. is playing in the street

Divide each of the following between the SUBJECT and PREDICATE with a double line (//); write your answer by putting the word on either side with the double line (//) in between.

20. The general // looked toward his troops.

21. All of the men on the left side // saluted.

22. On the right a different action // was taking place.

23. A private // was standing with his mouth open and eyes closed.

24. Others // did not tell him what was going on.

25. The general and his officers // did not laugh at the situation.

11

Lesson 2 **Nouns as Namers**

Nouns are a basic part of speech. In English they are the types of words which are used to give names to persons, places, and things. An easy way to remember what a **noun** does is to think of it **as a namer**.

Nouns are really quite arbitrary in the fact that new nouns can be made up for new things. The inventor or discoverer has a rather free choice of naming his new creation much as parents naming their newborn child. Once an item has been named, the name must gain acceptance, which it usually does. After the name is in general usage, it is quite difficult to change. Think about it; when a person says *DOG* or *CAT*, others think of what is generally agreed upon as a dog or a cat. Continually changing names would be confusing.

Names often have histories. Some names are made up from first letters of other words put together. *SONAR* comes from SOund NAvigation Ranging. This type of word has its own name, *ACRONYM*. Some names are made by combining two or three other names; *SONGBIRD* and *SISTER-IN-LAW* are two examples. *SOPHOMORE* is similar in that it is made from two Greek words, *SOPHOS* and *MOROS*, and altered a bit to fit English. Some names are from people themselves; *SILHOUETTE* is the last name of a former French minister of finance who did profile drawings. Sometimes we just borrow the word from some other language and make it sayable in English; *SQUASH* and *RACCOON* came from American Indian tongues.

NAMERS can be generally grouped into two categories: **PROPER** and **COMMON**.

❶ **Proper nouns** refer to a specific or particular individual or thing. They are always capitalized.

☞ Mary, Shakespeare, Friday, Thanksgiving, Chicago, America

❷ A **common noun** refers to any one of a class or group of beings or lifeless things or even the collection itself; also it can refer to a quality, action, condition, or general idea. They are only capitalized when beginning a sentence or when used as part of a title.

☞☞ girl, author, day, holiday, city, country, herd, tea

A subset of common nouns is classed as ABSTRACT nouns since they do not point to a real or concrete person, place, or thing. They are **abstract** in that they are **not tangible**; that is, they name things which **cannot be touched**. They are the opposite of the real or concrete nouns, those that can be touched.

☞ hardness, singing, serfdom, grammar, music, beauty, discipline
☞ honesty, love, fear, freedom, strength, faith, velocity, ability

Nouns as Namers Exercise 2

1. Give the primary function of a noun.
2. Explain how a proper noun can often be visually recognized from a common noun.
3. Give the subset or group of common nouns that refers to ideas and actions.
4. List the three general categories that nouns often name.
5. Name the part of the sentence that usually contains a noun.
6. Name the two parts of a basic simple sentence.
7. Identify the common end punctuation for basic sentences.
8. Give three of your own examples of proper nouns.
9. Give three of your own examples of abstract nouns.
10. Give three of your own examples of concrete common nouns.

Write the nouns found in each of the following sentences.

11. Henry went to the show with Jack.

12. A friend from California is staying for a week at our cabin this summer.

13. My brother was fishing from the bank of the river.

14. Our dad and mom allow two fishing trips per month.

15. Jill, Mary, and Hazel are now vacationing in upper Maine.

16-20. Divide each of the above five sentences between the SUBJECT and PREDICATE with a double line (//); write your answer by putting the word on either side with the double line (//) in between.

Supply a subject of your own for each of the following predicates.

21. ran to the windmill in his bare feet. (use 1 word)

22. had a good time eating ice cream. (use 3 words)

23. threw the ball with great skill. (use 5 words)

24. chased the cat into the culvert. (use 7 words)

25. tried to read a book in silence. (use 2 words)

> **DEFINITIONS**
> **SINGULAR** - the form of a noun representing one
> **PLURAL** - the form of a noun representing more than one
> **SUFFIX** - a syllable added to the end of a word
> **SIBILANT** - letters making a hissing sound (*s, sh, ch, x, z*)
> **INFLECTIONAL** - a change of form that alters meaning but not word type;
> shows some grammatical relationship: number, case, degree, etc.

Nouns are always namers, but they may exhibit other properties as well. Nouns can also show NUMBER. That means the noun can show whether it represents one or more than one. The **singular form** of a noun represents **one**. Through inflection a noun can be changed to represent **more than one**; we call that **plural**.

☞ singular = *boy*, (one)   ☞ plural = *boys*, (more than one)

Some nouns are measurable by different means than counting. They are counted in terms of some unit of measurement and are usually found in the singular form.

☞ *5 gallons of milk, 3 cups of water, 2 acres of corn*

❶ **Plurals are normally formed by adding the suffix *S* to the singular noun.**

☞ *boy-boys, hat-hats, barn-barns, dog-dogs, rivet-rivets*

❷ **A number of plurals are formed by adding the suffix *ES* under certain conditions.**

☞ The singular noun ends in a **sibilant** (*s, sh, ch, x, z*)
  ✎ *church-churches, dress-dresses, dish-dishes, box-boxes*

☞ The singular noun ends with a **consonant plus *Y*** (*Y* changes to *I*)
  ✎ *penny-pennies, lady-ladies, fly-flies*

☞ The singular noun **ends in *F* or *FE* and changes to *V***
  ✎ *wife-wives, wolf-wolves, dwarf-dwarves*
  However if no change from *F* to *V*, then just add *S*.
  ✎ *roof-roofs, gulf-gulfs, safe-safes*

☞ The singular noun **ends in *O* preceded by a consonant**
  This rule works only about half the time.
  ✎ *potato-potatoes, echo-echoes, tomato-tomatoes*
  BUT NOT *solo-solos, piano-pianos, casino-casinos*

☞ The singular noun **ends in *O* preceded by a vowel, just add *S***
  ✎ *bamboo-bamboos, folio-folios, curio-curios*

❸ **Some singular nouns form their plurals in an irregular manner.**

☞ *goose-geese, mouse-mice, foot-feet, man-men, child-children*

❹ **Some nouns have the same form for both singular and plural.**

☞ *deer, sheep, fowl, trout, salmon*

❺ **Some foreign words keep their foreign plurals.**

☞ *alumnus-alumni, phenomenon-phenomena*

❻ **The plurals of numbers, letters, signs, and words used as words out of context are formed by adding an apostrophe and an *S*.**

☞ 1980's, 6's, *m*'s, *k*'s, +'s, -'s, *and*'s, *but*'s

When in doubt about the formation of a plural, **consult a dictionary**; it gives irregular (non-*s*) forms.

Noun Plurals Exercise 3

1. How many does a plural form represent?
2. How many does a singular form represent?
3. Define *SUFFIX*.
4. Give the suffix most commonly used to form noun plurals.
5. Tell how the plurals of letters and numbers are formed.
6. Name the part of the sentence that usually contains a noun.
7. Name that part of the sentence that contains the main verb.
8. Tell what an inflected suffix does not change.
9. Give the term that means a letter standing for a hissing sound.

Form PLURALS for the following words.

10. hose	11. factory	12. half
13. stallion	14. fox	15. ditch
16. ablution	17. *if*	18. domino

Write the NOUNS found in each of the following sentences and label them S for SINGULAR or for PLURAL.

19. Seven boys from the team charged on the field at one time.

20. Henry used the oxen to move a load of rocks across the river.

21. A friend of my father fished the stream behind our house.

22. One sheep did not follow the other sheep into the pasture.

23. Terminal illness precluded his participation in the extravaganzas.

24. The tawdry mercenary imbibed choice juleps.

25-30. Divide each sentence above into SUBJECT and PREDICATE with a double line (//); write your answer by putting the word on either side with the double line (//) in between..

Lesson 4 Nouns: Possession

```
┌─────────────────────────────────────────┐
│              DEFINITION                   │
│                                           │
│         SYNTAX - word order               │
└─────────────────────────────────────────┘
```

Nouns are always namers as we have said before. Since nouns are entities of some sort, they can often own or be in some close association with other nouns. **The idea of ownership is labeled possession.** One noun can actually own or possess another noun.

There are two common ways of expressing this owner-owned relationship.

❶ One way is through the use of the word **OF**.

☞ a son *of* the king, a work *of* Shakespeare, author *of* the book

❷ The second common method of expressing the same relationship is **inflect the owning noun**. The INFLECTIONAL ending for nouns is the APOSTROPHE; the letter *S* is added after the APOSTROPHE if an **additional *S* sound is heard**. Singular words almost always add the *S*; plurals generally do if they don't end in *S* already.

☞ SINGULAR				☞ PLURAL		
boy	*dog*	*man*		*boys*	*dogs*	*men*
boy's	*dog's*	*man's*	POSSESSIVE	*boys'*	*dogs'*	*men's*

The rule is simple: **ADD an '** (apostrophe) to form the possessive, and **ADD an *S* if the EXTRA SOUND is heard**. Two sibilants in a row are fine, but English doesn't allow three sibilants in a row.

☞ *mass - mass's*   *masses - masses'*   *Amos - Amos's*   *Jesus - Jesus'*

Compound possessives occur when two or more people have a common ownership or association with the same noun. In this case **only the last owning noun shows the possession** for all of the nouns.

☞ John and Bill's car   (They own it together.)
☞ Fred, Henry, and Carl's dad   (They have the same father.)

The whole concept of one noun closely associating with another noun is labeled **GENITIVE** by the grammarian. POSSESSION is the major relationship expressed, but other ideas are represented by the genitive as well:

☞ origin (*warrior's deeds*)   ☞ material (*idol of gold*)
☞ composition (*flock of birds*)   ☞ characteristic (*child's language*)
☞ measure (*an hour's delay*)   ☞ apposition (*gift of song*)
☞ whole from which a part is taken (*piece of bread*).

A double genitive can occur. This happens when the *OF* form is used as well as the *'S* form.

☞ a suggestion of Sam's, a bone of Fido's, a throne of the king's

Certain expressions show their genitive relationship strictly through syntax by compounding and have no inflected form or do not use an *OF* construction.

☞ sunrise (rising of the sun), earthquake (quaking of the earth)

Nouns: Possession

1. Give the possessive inflectional ending for singular nouns.
2. Give the possessive inflectional ending for plural nouns ending in *S*.
3. Give the word used in a phrase to show a genitive relationship between two nouns.
4. Give the possessive inflectional ending of a plural noun not ending in *S*.
5. Define *SYNTAX*.
6. Define *SIBILANT*.
7. Define *SUFFIX*.
8. Give the name for a noun that tells what it does.
9. Tell what an inflected suffix changes for a word.

Form PLURALS of the following words.

10. box	11. church	12. fly
13. dwarf	14. hostage	15. tooth

16-21. Form POSSESSIVES for both the singular and plurals of each of the above.

Divide each sentence below into SUBJECT and PREDICATE with a double line (//); write your answer in the usual fashion.

22. Carlos became the foreman in the bakery after ten months of work.

23. The bread from the ovens in the morning smelled tremendously good.

24. Five of the youngsters on the block came to the bakery each morning.

25. The children enjoyed the smell of the freshly baked bread.

Supply a SUBJECT of your own for each of the following predicates.

26. slithered into the forest.   (2 words, use a possessive)

27. threw the ball into the pond.   (6 words)

28. fell over the chair.   (3 words, use a possessive)

29. ate scrambled eggs for dinner.   (4 words, use a compound possessive)

30. felt sick after eating grass.   (5 words)

DEFINITION

DERIVATIONAL - a change of form that alters both the meaning and the word type

---

Suffixes come in **two basic types:** INFLECTIONAL and DERIVATIONAL. Both types change the meaning of words, but only the derivational type will change the type of word from one to another.

The **SYNTAX RULE** in English is that the **last derivational suffix** on a word **determines** its **class** or what type of word it is. If inflectional and derivational suffixes are used together on the same word, the **inflectional** suffix will **always come last** since it **does not affect the word class**.

    ☞ govern**ments**   *ment* = derivational suffix   *s* = inflectional suffix

Thus we see that a noun formed by the addition of a derivational suffix can show possession or plurality in the same manner as a noun which has no derivational suffix. The rule of order also applies to the two noun inflectional suffixes. It should be obvious that if both types, plural and possession, occur, then the plural will be first, and the possessive comes last.

All suffixes have meaning of some kind. Previously we have seen that suffixes show number or a genitive relationship. Derivational suffixes have a variety of meanings. Fortunately, the derivational suffixes tend to differentiate themselves by word class; that is, a suffix with a noun meaning signifies a noun and nothing else.

One group of noun suffixes has the meaning of *little* and often expresses some endearment. These are called **diminutive endings**. Suffixes of this sort follow below.

    ☞ *-KIN, -LING, -ETTE, -LET, -IE,* and *-Y.*

    ✍ lambkin, gosling, kitchenette, rivulet, Katie, kitty

A second group of noun suffixes has the meaning of *one who*.

    ☞ *-AN, -AR, -(Y)ER, -OR, -IST,* and *-ITE*

    ✍ Christian, liar, lawyer, conductor, violinist, Israelite

A third group of noun suffixes has the meaning of *state, condition,* or *quality of.*

    ☞ *-DOM, -HOOD, -ION, -ISM, -MENT, -NESS, -SHIP, -TY*

    ✍ kingdom, childhood, extension, humanism, argument, kindness, stewardship, frivolity

NOTE: The above list is not inclusive; there are other noun derivational suffixes, and some of the suffixes above may have alternative meanings depending upon use. Knowing the meanings of derivational suffixes helps a person learn the meanings of words. Not all nouns have derivational suffixes, but many do. The suffixes are important to know and learn. Nouns can be made from other types of words with the use of derivational suffixes. Noun derivational suffixes can also be added on to other nouns.

    ☞ happy   happiness   (adjective becomes noun)
    ☞ invent   inventor   (verb becomes noun)
    ☞ king   kingdom   (noun stays noun)

Nouns: Derivational Suffixes Exercise 5

1. Give the type of word that is usually found in the subject.
2. Give the type of word that normally begins a predicate.
3. The subject of a sentence is also called the (?) part.
4. The predicate of a sentence is also called the (?) part.
5. Name the suffix type which changes the meaning not class or type.
6. Name the suffix type which changes both the meaning and the class of a word.
7. Give two examples of a diminutive ending for nouns.
8. Give three examples of noun derivational suffixes that mean *ONE WHO*.
9. Give three examples of noun derivational suffixes that mean *QUALITY OF*.
10. Define *PLURAL*.

Form PLURAL POSSESSIVES for each of the following words.

      11. calf   12. girl   13. child

Make a NOUN by adding a DERIVATIONAL SUFFIX to each of the following words.

      14. cigar   15. rule   16. sad

      17. violin   18. extend   19. equivocate

Write the NOUNS found in the sentences below and label them *S* for singular and *P* for plural.

20. Folmer and Harald requested privacy from the other prisoners.

21. The two men were not excited about their prospects for the future.

22. The roving band of highwaymen had caught the brothers by surprise.

23. At the thieves' camp the living conditions were quite poor.

24. The brothers hoped to gain some comfort by being alone.

25. Their plans did not materialize and bear fruit, however.

26-31. Divide each sentence above into SUBJECT and PREDICATE with a double line (//).

Lesson 6   Noun Functions 1

DEFINITIONS

BASEWORD - also HEADWORD, the word which serves as the focus
for other words in a group
CLUSTER - a group of words all centering around a baseword
MODIFY - to limit or qualify
SIMPLE SUBJECT - the noun baseword of the cluster serving as subject
in a sentence

Nouns are very useful in sentences. Most nouns can do any of **six various jobs in a sentence**, but any given noun can do **only one job at a time**. One of the jobs that a noun can do is to modify another noun. The **syntax is always the same** when this occurs; the **modifier precedes the noun being modified**.

☞ brick wall (*brick* modifies *wall*), Mary's horse (*Mary* modifies *horse*)

You will note that the POSSESSIVE FORM is one common way that one noun modifies or qualifies another. This function is somewhat different from other noun functions in that the noun modifier is not central to the meaning of the sentence and may be dropped with only a slight loss of meaning to the sentence. The **modifier is not essential to the basic meaning** of the sentence.

☞ He ran into a brick wall.   ☞ He ran into a wall.

A noun functioning in any other capacity is much more important to the meaning of its sentence and cannot be dropped without making the sentence incomplete or altering the meaning greatly.

A very common function of a noun is that of SIMPLE SUBJECT of a sentence. We know that all basic sentences are composed of a subject and predicate. We also know that the subject can be as small as one word or expanded to many words.

☞ Dogs // barked.   ☞ The very loud dogs from down the block // barked.

In the first sentence of the example, the **simple subject is the complete subject, *dogs***. In the second sentence the **simple subject is still *dogs*, but the complete subject is all the words to the left of the double line (//)**. ☞ Note that all the other words in the subject of the second sentence cluster around the baseword *dogs*; those other words generally point to the baseword.

Most of the time **finding the simple subject of a sentence is just a matter of picking out the main noun to which the other words point.** Eliminating extra words like adjectives & prepositional phrases helps.

There are instances where there is more than one simple subject in a sentence. This occurs when two or more nouns are connected by the **coordinating conjunctions *AND* or *OR***. Two nouns sharing the subject position are called **compound subjects**.

☞ The dog and the cat chased the rat.

Both *dog* and *cat* are the simple subjects of the sentence since they are equally yoked with the word *and*.

20

Noun Functions 1   Exercise 6

1. Give the term for the single word that a complete subject can be reduced to.
2. Name the type of word (word class) that the single word in question one must be.
3. Explain what compound subjects are.
4. When a noun can be thrown out of the sentence with little loss of meaning, what is the function of the noun being thrown out?
5. Give the possessive inflectional ending for singular nouns.
6. Give the meaning for the noun derivational endings -*MENT* and -*NESS*.
7. How does a sibilant on the end of a singular noun affect the forming of plurals?
8. Give the one word meaning for noun derivational diminutive endings.
9. List any three noun derivational endings which mean *ONE WHO*.
10. Explain the relationship between a cluster and a baseword.

Form PLURALS for the following words.

    11. roof   12. *Q*   13. radish

Add a NOUN DERIVATIONAL ENDING to each of the following words.

    14. prison   15. brother   16. history

    17. argue   18. dine   19. frivolous

Divide each sentence below into SUBJECT and PREDICATE with a double line (//). Then write the SIMPLE SUBJECTS.

20. Fifty feet from the entrance the tunnel turned sharply to the right.

21. The two boys and their dog moved quietly along the right edge.

22. The lead boy held a flashlight and played its beam ahead of them.

23. Suddenly the circle of light moving on the floor vanished into space.

24. The apprehension rose in both of the boys quite rapidly.

25. From the looks of it the floor fell off into nothing.

Make up various SUBJECTS for the following predicate: *fell through space.*

26. use three words
27. use five words, simple subject = a noun with a derivational ending
28. use four words, a compound subject
29. use one word only
30. use seven words

Lesson 7   <u>Noun Markers</u>

A **noun marker (NM)** is a word that **marks a noun**; it points to a noun that follows, often the very next word. **Asking the question WHO or WHAT following a NM will reveal the noun being marked.**

Noun markers are made up of some words commonly known as adjectives and pronouns. Some grammarians call the pronouns pronominal adjectives. We will just call them all noun markers in this text.

The first group of NM's we will consider are the **most common**; only **three words** comprise this group. They are also called **ARTICLES**. The words are *A, AN*, and *THE*. *AN* is normally used prior to words beginning with a VOWEL SOUND while *A* precedes words starting with a CONSONANT SOUND.

☞ an egg, an icicle, an hour   ☞ a door, a cow, a big oak

☞ **NOTE:** The use of *A* or *AN* is dependent upon the very next word, not necessarily the noun it points to.

The second group of NM's is a group that indicates some QUANTITY. These words can be very **definite** such as numbers **or** rather **indefinite**.

☞ one boy, two boys, some boys, no boys, many boys

The following list contains **most** of the **common indefinite NM's**.

ALL	ANY	BOTH	EACH	EITHER	EVERY
FEW	MANY	MORE	MOST	MUCH	NEITHER
NO	SEVERAL	SOME	SUCH		

A third group of NM's is the PRONOMINAL ADJECTIVES, pronouns that in some way modify the noun. This group breaks into **two general types**, the **demonstratives** and certain **possessives**.

☞ DEMONSTRATIVE: THIS   THAT   THESE   THOSE.

☞ POSSESSIVE: MY   OUR   YOUR   HIS
          HER   ITS   THEIR   THY

The NM does not stand alone; it needs the noun in order to be complete. Again, the easy way to find the noun being pointed to is to say the NM and ask WHO or WHAT; the word answering the question will be the noun.

☞ the old rusty bucket sitting on a stump

☞ NM (the) + WHAT? = the bucket

Thus, *bucket* is the noun marked or pointed to by *the*, the NM in this phrase.

☞ **NOTE:** Nouns may occur with or without NM's marking them; in fact, some nouns, especially proper names, rarely have NM's associated with them.

☞ Alice ate two eggs for her breakfast.   ☞ Alice ate eggs for breakfast.

Noun Markers

1. Explain what a noun marker does.
2. List the three most common NM's.
3. Define *SYNTAX*.
4. List four examples of NM's that show indefinite quantities.
5. List the four NM's that are demonstrative pronouns.
6. Give the syntax rule for NM's and the nouns they mark.
7. List the two basic types of suffixes.
8. List the two parts of every basic sentence.
9. Give the ending for plural possessives that end in *S*.
10. Give the ending for plurals of letters, numbers, and signs.

Form PLURAL POSSESSIVES for each of the following words.

11. man   12. dress   13. scout

Add a NOUN DERIVATIONAL ENDING to each of the following words.

14. Christ   15. solemn   16. dive

Divide each sentence below between the SUBJECT and PREDICATE in the usual manner; then write the SIMPLE SUBJECTS.

17. The two feisty dogs played together in the yard.

18. Over near the back fence the clothesline sagged close to the ground.

19. Their master's new shirt whipping in the wind was a real temptation.

20. Fido and Bruno had a great time pulling on the shirt.

21. Unfortunately for them the shirt was not intended to be their toy.

22. Of course the dogs did not foresee the problems ahead.

Make up various SUBJECTS for the following PREDICATE: *blasted through the doorway*.

23. use two words, one a demonstrative NM
24. use three words, one a possessive NM
25. use four words; have a compound subject
26. use three words, one an indefinite NM
27. use five words, one simple subject with two NM's
28. use one word

Lesson 8

A test frame is a sentence with a blank in it. In the noun test frame, the blank can be filled by any noun. Here is the noun test frame we will use.

        NOUN TEST FRAME   ☞ (The) _____ is/are good.

Note that the first word, *the*, is in parenthesis; this means that it may or may not occur depending upon the needs of the noun filling the blank. For instance, we would not say, "The Mary is good;" we would say, "Mary is good." It should also be noted that a choice of *is* or *are* is available, again in order to accommodate the needs of the noun.

        ☞ Boys are good.   ☞ The boy is good.

The point is to use those words in the test frame that best fit the word placed in the blank so as to have the sentence make sense and sound correct.

A word of caution about test frames is in order. The noun test frame will **only tell us** that the word in question **could be used** as a noun, not that it is always a noun. The same holds true for the other test frames as well. If a word fits into the frame, it only means that the word could be used as that particular type of word, not that it always is that type of word.

      VERB TEST FRAME   ☞ Let's _____ (it).

      ADJECTIVE TEST FRAME   ☞ She/it seemed _____.

For illustration let us consider four words: *CAT, CREAMY, EAT,* and *LIGHT.*

Now we will put each word into each test frame.

CAT	The cat is good.	Let's cat it.	It seemed cat.
CREAMY	The creamy is good.	Let's creamy it.	It seemed creamy.
EAT	The eat is good.	Let's eat it.	It seemed eat.
LIGHT	The light is good.	Let's light it.	It seemed light.

Note that the first three only fit well into one test frame; thus, we can surmise they are that type of word. *CAT* is a **noun**; *CREAMY* is an **adjective**, and *EAT* is a **verb**. *LIGHT*, however, fits in all three just fine and could, therefore, be used as a noun, verb, or adjective depending upon the conditions of the sentence in which it appears. The test frame then can be used in two ways: to eliminate possibilities and to establish probabilities. In the above, *cat* could not be a verb or adjective, but it could be a noun.

Test Frames

1. Briefly explain the function of a test frame.
2. Give the term meaning that two nouns are both the subject.
3. Give the possessive inflectional ending for singular nouns.
4. Give the plural inflectional ending for nouns ending in a sibilant.
5. Give the term for the word which functions as the main word in a cluster of words focusing on that word.
6. Give the meaning for the noun derivational endings *-IST* and *-ER*.
7. List the three most common noun markers.
8. Give the two parts of every basic sentence.
9. Give the term which means *WORD ORDER*.
10. Give the term which means a syllable added to the end of a word.

Use the TEST FRAMES and list the possible word class(es) of the following words.

11. winterize	12. argonaut	13. fulsome
14. fish	15. obverse	16. pedometer
17. hammer	18. sound	

Form POSSESSIVES of the following words.

19. Olga	20. girls
21. ox	22. lass

Divide each sentence into SUBJECT and PREDICATE in the usual manner.

23. Bolman and Figuero hastened to the waiting boat.

24. The men cast furtive glances over their shoulders almost continuously.

25. From the darkness of an alley behind the men, a moaning filled the air.

26. Evidence of foul play was beginning to rear its ugly head.

27-30. Write all the NOUNS in each of the sentences above.

31-34. Write the SIMPLE SUBJECTS of each sentence above.

Lesson 9 **Pronouns**

Traditional grammar identifies a class of words as PRONOUNS; it further defines the class as **words that take the place of nouns**. This text will deal with pronouns in a slightly different manner. You have already seen in Lesson 7 that **some pronouns function as NM's**; they are the ones called **pronominal adjectives** by some. They are called such because they function in the manner of a modifier of the noun. The list in Lesson 7 contains those pronominal pronouns but puts them under the classifications of **demonstratives**, **indefinites**, and **certain possessive personals**.

The rest of the traditional pronouns function as nouns in that they are able to stand alone without a noun beside them and be full substitutes for nouns in their non-modification functions. **This text will simply treat these pronouns as a special class of nouns**.

The bulk of the pronouns which function as nouns instead of NM's are classified as **personal pronouns**. **There are THREE PERSONS, THREE BASIC CASES, THREE GENDERS, and SINGULAR and PLURAL NUMBER represented by the group called personal pronouns.**

☞ FIRST PERSON is the person speaking: *I, ME, WE*, and others.
☞ SECOND PERSON is the person spoken to: *YOU.*
☞ THIRD PERSON is the person spoken about: *HE, HER, THEM, IT*, and others.

The three **cases are subject** or nominative, **object** or accusative, and **possessive** or genitive. The three **genders are masculine, feminine**, and **neuter** and **only** show up in the **third person singular forms. Number,** you will remember, is one or more than one, **singular** and **plural**. The chart below will help.

PERSONAL PRONOUNS - CASE			
		SUBJECTIVE (Nominative)	OBJECTIVE (Accusative)	POSSESSIVE (Genitive)
person	number			
1st	(s)	I	me	mine, (my)
	(pl)	we	us	ours, (our)
2nd	(s)	you	you	yours, (your)
	*old	thou	thee	thine, (thy)
	(pl)	you	you	yours, (your)
	*old	ye	ye	
3rd gender{	(s) (m)	he	him	his
	(f)	she	her	hers, (her)
	(n)	it	it	its
	(pl)	they	them	theirs, (their)

☞ **NOTE 1:** the forms in parentheses in the possessive column are used as NM's.
☞ **NOTE 2:** the *thou* forms are always capitalized when referring to the Godhead.

Pronouns Exercise 9

1. Give the two word classes that a traditional pronoun can function as.
2. Give the first person plural objective form of the personal pronoun.
3. Give another name for the subjective case.
4. Give another name for the objective case.
5. Give the old form of *YOU* in the plural subjective case.
6. Give the word that is used to show possession in a phrase.
7. Explain the use of *A* and *AN*.
8. List any three indefinite pronouns.
9. Define *SYNTAX*.
10. List the two basic types of endings found on form words.

Form PLURALS of the following words.

    11. scarf   12. flurry   13. crutch

Form POSSESSIVES of the following words.

    14. Hal and Joe   15. foreigners   16. Elmer Jones

Add a NOUN DERIVATIONAL SUFFIX to each of the following words.

    17. work   18. America   19. yellow

Divide each sentence below into SUBJECT and PREDICATE in the usual manner.

20. The horses and wagons from the mountains now came in a steady stream.

21. The local cowboys from the valley watched them come with indifference.

22. Movers were no longer new or different after the first wave.

23. The folks riding in the wagons and tending to the train did not stop.

24. The lure of the good land to the far west compelled them to go on.

25-29. Write all the NOUNS in each sentence above.

30-34. Write the SIMPLE SUBJECTS of each sentence above.

Lesson 10   Prepositions

The **preposition is a function word** or a structure word. It is used to glue other words together, usually two nouns.

The preposition will show either a **time or a space relationship**. **Most prepositions show a space relationship.** An easy way to see if a word is a space type preposition is to see if it fits a simple test. Think of a kite and a cloud. Anywhere that kite can be in relationship to the cloud is prepositional.

The TEST FRAME for SPACE RELATIONAL PREPOSITIONS is below.

    ☞ The kite flew _____ the cloud(s). *through   in   inside*

Prepositions do not exist by themselves; they are a part of a phrase. The prepositional phrase (Pp) may consist of as few as two words, the PREPOSITION and its OBJECT (OP). Often other words occur between the preposition and its object; the most common is a noun marker.

            P   OP   P   OP   P   OP
    ☞ to town, at home, in the water, near the shore, to the store

Any words which might fit into a noun cluster in front of a noun can be a part of a prepositional phrase. Adjectives are the other most common type of word which occur in prepositional phrases.

We drove   *P   OP*
    ☞ in the red truck, (over the big wall)

The **first word** in a prepositional phrase is **always a preposition;** the **last word** in the phrase is **always the object of the preposition.** Everything that occurs between the two is part of that prepositional phrase. The **formula for a prepositional phrase is P + ... + OP.** The **...** represents anything that comes between

An easy way to find the object of the preposition is to say the preposition and ask the question *WHAT?* The word that answers the question will be object of that preposition.

    ☞ in the house --- in what?   *house* = OP

There are a few time relational prepositions. TIME PREPOSITIONS fit into a different TEST FRAME.

    ☞ _____ the game she slept.

NOTE 1: Some words that are prepositions can also function as adverbs. The key is to see if the word has an object or not. **Prepositions have objects;** adverbs do not have objects.
NOTE 2: At times certain words may switch classes. *FOR* can be either a preposition or a coordinating conjunction. *BEFORE* and *AFTER* can be subordinators or prepositions. Only when functioning as prepositions will they have objects.
NOTE 3: *TO* followed by a simple form of a verb is part of an infinitive and is never a preposition in that case. When using *TO*, always check to see if a verb or an object follows; this will determine word class.

    ☞ He ran outside.   (*outside* = adverb, tells where)
    ☞ He ran outside the house.   (*outside* = preposition, has object)
    ☞ He ran after he walked.   (*after* = subordinator, connects two ideas)
    ☞ He ran after the horse.   (*after* = preposition, has object)
    ☞ He ran to save his house.   (*to* = infinitive, verb follows)
    ☞ He ran to his house.   (*to* = preposition, has object)

Prepositions Exercise 10

Make a list of prepositions. Use the two test frames and the kite and cloud idea. The letters given are the first letters of the words.

A	B	I	T
_____	_____	_____	_____
_____	_____	_____	_____
_____	_____	_____	_____
_____	_____	N	_____
_____	_____	_____	_____
_____	_____	O	U
_____	_____	_____	_____
_____	_____	_____	_____
_____	D	_____	_____
_____	_____	_____	_____
_____	_____	_____	_____
	_____	_____	W
	F	_____	_____
	_____	S	_____
	_____	_____	

NOTE 1: In the answers, words with the * are the five most common prepositions. You should identify them on this paper in the same fashion after you finish.

NOTE 2: One very common preposition does not fit either test frame and must be memorized because it occurs very often. It is the word *OF*.

[See Additional Exercises, pages 161-163 for more practice.]

Lesson 11 Verb Types

Verbs are the **telling words** of the language. Just as nouns are namers, so verbs are tellers. Verbs are commonly found in the PREDICATE part of the sentence. In fact, a verb usually begins the predicate.

Verbs fall into **two basic types**, ACTIVE (V) and LINKING (LV). The **easiest way to tell the two types apart** is to **MEMORIZE THE LINKING VERBS**. There are **only twelve basic linking verbs**; all the other verbs in English are active. In unusual situations, certain normally active verbs may be used as linking verbs, but such use is rare.

The **COMMON LINKING VERBS** are listed below in their simple forms.

BE	**BECOME**	**REMAIN**			
LOOK	**APPEAR**	**TASTE**	**SMELL**	**SOUND**	**FEEL**
ACT	**GROW**	*SEEM*			

The **linking verbs** are also called **state of being verbs**. They do not represent action but rather state an observation or a judgment of a condition.

   ☞ He looks funny.   ☞ The water is cold.   ☞ My dog seems sick.

You will note that the above examples reflect some observation or judgment on the part of the speaker about the subject of the sentence. To see the real difference between active and linking verbs, note the two examples below.

   ☞ He felt funny.   ☞ He felt a cold wind.

The first example represents a judgment or observation about the subject; it is linking. The second example tells what the subject did; it is active. ☞ **NOTE:** The word *felt* can be linking or active. It is a verb from the second row of the list; those verbs are **sensory** in nature and can be active or linking; it depends on how they are used.

The three words in the first row all describe a state of being or existence. They state a condition that **already is** (*be*), **is coming into being** (*become*), or **is staying in existence** (*remain*).

The first two words in the last row are similar to those in the second row in that they can be active or linking, but *seem* **is always linking**.

Again, the basic difference in the active and linking verbs is one of FUNCTION. The **linking verbs link** a quality or condition or state of being in the subject complement to the subject. The **active verbs tell** what the subject is doing.

☞ **NOTE:** There are **over 100,000 verbs** in English, but **only 12 are commonly linking**. It is essential to know the difference between linking and active verbs in many cases. Know the 12 and their forms; everything not linking must then be active. Do yourself a big favor and **memorize them now**.

Verb Types

1. Give the verb which is always linking.
2. In which part of the sentence do verbs usually occur?
3. Which of the two types of verbs is the biggest group of verbs?
4. Give the function of a linking verb.
5. Give the function of an active verb.
6. List the five common prepositions.
7. List the three most common noun markers.
8. Give the first person singular nominative personal pronoun form.
9. Define *SIBILANT*.
10. Give the possessive inflectional ending for a singular noun.

Form PLURALS of the following words.

    11. goose   12. moose   13. noose

Form POSSESSIVES of the following words.

    14. Joe Burns   15. dogs   16. farm

Add a DERIVATIONAL SUFFIX to form a noun of each of the following words.

    17. play   18. institute   19. mother

Divide each sentence into SUBJECT and PREDICATE in the usual manner.

20. Filmore chased the pig around a stack of hay and into the barn.

21. That pig was fast and crafty as well as slippery.

22. In the dim light of the barn the pig slipped away into the darkness.

23. The air was filled with smells of leather, manure, and hay.

24. The porker hid himself in a dark corner under some old straw.

25-29. Write all the NOUNS in the sentences above.

30-34. Write all the VERBS in the sentences above.

35-39. Write all the PREPOSITIONAL PHRASES (Pp's) in the sentences above.

Lesson 12 Verb Forms

```
DEFINITIONS

REGULAR VERB - a verb which uses -ED for its past forms
IRREGULAR VERB - a verb that doesn't form its past forms regularly
```

Both active and linking verbs have inflected forms. **Almost all verbs have a SIMPLE or BASE form and FOUR INFLECTED FORMS.** The verb *BE*, however, has **eight forms** altogether. The forms follow:

BE   AM   IS   ARE   WAS   WERE   BEING   BEEN

These forms should be MEMORIZED so that the *BE* verb in any form is recognized on sight. As you can see, this verb is very irregular.

All other verbs, excepting MODALS, form their two present forms similarly. The -*S* form adds *S* or *ES* to the simple form depending on spelling and pronunciation needs. The -*ING* form always adds *ING*.

☞ walk, walks, walking   ☞ go, goes, going   ☞ drive, drives, driving

The FORMS and TEST FRAMES to derive them are given in the chart below.

VERB FORM	ALSO CALLED	TEST FRAME
SIMPLE form	**Present** First Person Singular	Today I _____.
-*S* form	**Present** Third Person Singular	Today he _____.
-*ING* form	**Present** Participle	I am _____.
-*ED* form	**Past,** Simple or Narrative Past	Yesterday I ____.
-*EN* form	**Past** Participle	I have _____.

A good deal of variety occurs in the PAST TENSE FORMS. Distinguishing between regular and irregular verbs in the -*ED* form and the -*EN* form is important. Regular verbs do things in a regular manner, and most verbs in English are regular. The two past forms, the -*ED* and -*EN* forms, BOTH ADD -*ED* IF THE VERB IS REGULAR. IRREGULAR VERBS do many and various things to make these two forms; some add other letters; some change internally, and some do nothing at all.

☞ (regular) walked, walked   ☞ (irregular) ate, eaten; sang, sung; put, put; buy, bought

ITEMS TO NOTE
1) Both **participle forms** exist as **true verbs only when a form of *BE* or *HAVE* is present**.
2) The two past tense forms of a regular verb look exactly alike.
3) Many irregular verbs have a family that makes past tense forms in a similar manner.
    ☞ drove, driven; rode, ridden   ☞ sang, sung; drank, drunk   ☞ fought, fought; caught, caught
4) The verb *BE* has EIGHT FORMS instead of the usual five.
5) Irregular forms usually have the endings given in the dictionary under the basic or root word entry.
6) Use the test frames to hear the various forms. Today I weep. Yesterday I wept. I have wept.

Verb Forms

1. Give the type of word that is usually found in the subject.
2. Give the type of word that normally begins a predicate.
3. Give the verb type which makes its past forms by adding -*ED*.
4. Give the ending of the present participle verb form.
5. Give the ending of the third person singular present verb form.
6. Write the verb which is always linking.
7. Give the eight forms of *BE*.
8. Give the second person singular subject personal pronoun form.
9. Give the three most common noun markers.
10. List the two items which always occur in a prepositional phrase.

Form PLURALS of the following words.

    11. cave   12. mess   13. trout

Form POSSESSIVES of the following words.

    14. cats   15. dog   16. Sherlock Holmes

Add a DERIVATIONAL SUFFIX to form a NOUN of each of the following words.

    17. flute   18. connect   19. wise

Give the FOUR OTHER FORMS for each verb listed below.

    20. run   21. jump   22. fight

Divide each sentence below into SUBJECT and PREDICATE in the usual manner.

23. Sir Cos and Sir Balwain entered the dark passage ahead of the others.

24. The two men wore heavy armor and had their swords out and ready.

25. The legend of the castle and its dangers worried them.

26. A single mistake could cost them their lives in an instant.

27. The adventure did not seem so glorious right at this moment.

28-32. Write all the PREPOSITIONAL PHRASES (Pp's) in the sentences above.

33-37. Write all the NOUNS in the sentences above.

38-42. Write all the VERBS in the sentences above.

[See Additional Exercises, page 164 for more practice on verb forms.]

```
┌─────────────────────────────────────────────────────────────────┐
│                          DEFINITIONS                              │
│                                                                   │
│        AUXILIARY VERB - a verb which helps the main verb          │
│  VERB BASEWORD - the main verb in a cluster of verbs and other modifiers │
└─────────────────────────────────────────────────────────────────┘
```

The **auxiliary verb is NOT a main verb**; the **main verb carries the meaning** while the **auxiliary verb modifies or helps** the meaning in some way. There are THREE BASIC AUXILIARY VERBS: *BE*, *HAVE*, and *DO*. In addition to these verbs and their various forms, a special subclass of verbs called **MODALS also function as auxiliary verbs**.

In active voice when the *BE* forms function as auxiliary verbs, they are **always followed by an -*ING* form**.

☞ was running   ☞ is walking   ☞ been going   ☞ am eating

When the *HAVE* forms function as auxiliary verbs, they are **always followed by an -*EN* form**.

☞ have walked   ☞ has eaten   ☞ had thrown

When the *DO* forms function as auxiliary verbs, they are **always followed by a SIMPLE form**. When *DO* is used in this manner, it is used for emphasis.

☞ do walk   ☞ did eat   ☞ does go

☞ **NOTE:** Each of the above can be used as a **main verb**.

☞ He was happy.   ☞ She has fun.   ☞ It did the job.

The **KEY** to deciding if a verb is an auxiliary or not **is to see if a verb follows directly behind and is in the correct form**.

MODALS are somewhat different from other verbs in that they **only have two forms**, a present and a past. There are **only nine modals**.

```
┌─────────────────────────────────────────────────────────────────┐
│   CAN        SHALL       WILL        MAY         MUST             │
│   COULD      SHOULD      WOULD       MIGHT                        │
└─────────────────────────────────────────────────────────────────┘
```

When these words function as auxiliary verbs, they are **always followed by a simple form**. Modals show probability or possibility; they lend a degree of uncertainty.

☞ may go   ☞ will eat   ☞ might run   ☞ should fly   ☞ must begin

☞ **NOTE:** Of the modals, **only *CAN* and *WILL* can be used as main verbs**, and then they will have a meaning different from their modal sense.

☞ She canned the peaches.   ☞ He willed his dog a fortune.

Auxiliary Verbs Exercise 13

1. List the three basic auxiliary verbs.
2. List any five modals.
3. Give the verb form which always follows a modal.
4. Give the verb form which always follows a *BE* auxiliary verb.
5. Give the ending of the past participle verb form.
6. List any four linking verbs in simple form.
7. Give the past forms of *BE*.
8. Give the third person plural object personal pronoun form.
9. Give the three most common noun markers.
10. Give the common preposition beginning with *O*.

Form PLURALS of the following words.

    11. chair   12. hutch   13. foot

Form POSSESSIVES of the following words.

    14. cows   15. Jim and Bob   16. Robert Burns

Add a DERIVATIONAL SUFFIX to form a NOUN of each of the following words.

    17. dark   18. friend   19. warm

Give the FOUR OTHER FORMS for each verb listed below.

    20. steal   21. charge   22. drink

Divide each sentence below into SUBJECT and PREDICATE in the usual manner.

23. The two knights halted at a sharp corner and incline of the passage.

24. A soft green slime and a putrid odor had now become evident.

25. Clearly the danger of the descent was becoming greater and greater.

26. Slowly and carefully the men peered around the corner.

27. A series of steps descended into the black of nothingness before them.

28-32. Write all the PREPOSITIONAL PHRASES (Pp's) in the sentences above.

33-37. Write all the NOUNS in the sentences above.

38-42. Write all the VERBS in the sentences above.

Lesson 14 <u>Verb Cluster Syntax</u>

A verb cluster (Vcl) is formed around a verb baseword (Vbw); **the cluster always follows a very rigid order**. The syntax formula is shown immediately below.

```
MODAL  ( + simple )  HAVE  ( + en )  BE  ( + ing )  Vbw
```

	M	HAVE	BE	Vbw			M	HAVE	BE	Vbw
He				runs.		He				ran.
He			is	running.		He			was	running.
He		has		run.		He		had		run.
He	may			run.		He	might			run.
He	may		be	running.		He	might		be	running
He	may	have		run.		He	might	have		run.
He		has	been	running.		He		had	been	running.
He	may	have	been	running.		He	might	have	been	running.

The left column above is present tense while the right column is past tense. All possible variations of active voice constructions are given except *DO* forms. It should be noted that the *DO* forms only exist in one construction, the auxiliary *DO* and the simple form of the Vbw behind it.

☞ **ITEMS TO NOTE:** 1) The **Vbw** is **always** the **last verb** in the cluster.
2) The **first verb** in a cluster **shows tense** and **agrees with the subject**.
3) The order is rigid and never varies in the active voice.

Knowing the definitive order of verb clusters allows one to identify the complete verb cluster somewhat easily. **First** it is necessary to **know the forms of *HAVE, BE*, and the Modals** on sight. **Next**, since each auxiliary requires a certain form to follow it, the procedure is simply to **look to the right** and find the requisite forms until the Vbw is identified.

Other words will appear in a verb cluster. These words are **not verbs**, **but** they **are** a **part of the Vcl.**

   1) Negatives usually appear in the form of *NOT* and show up after the first verb in a Vcl.

      ☞ He may not run.   ☞ They had not been eating for long.

   2) Verb modifiers (adverbs) may occur within the Vcl.

      ☞ He may have still run.   ☞ She may always have been my friend.

☞ **NOTE:** The actual placement of the adverbs is somewhat up to the writer.

☞ He still may have run.   ☞ He may still have run.   ☞ He may have still run.

☞ **NOTE:** A sentence can have more than one main verb; these are called **compound verbs**.

☞ He ate his supper and went to bed.   ☞ The dog bristled, growled, and charged.

Verb Cluster Syntax Exercise 14

1. List the three main auxiliary types in their Vcl syntax order.
2. List any four modals.
3. List the present forms of *BE*.
4. List the present forms of *HAVE*.
5. Give the three most common noun markers.
6. Give the plural possessive form for most words.
7. Give the second person plural nominative pronoun form.
8. List the present tense form of a verb that requires an auxiliary.
9. Give the term which means a syllable added to the end of a word.
10. Give the term that means *WORD ORDER*.

Form PLURALS of the following words.

    11. camel   12. fox   13. ox

Form POSSESSIVES of the following words.

    14. Jim Carnes   15. Dan and Bill   16. movies

Add a NOUN DERIVATIONAL SUFFIX to each of the following words.

    17. impress   18. friend   19. operate

Give the FOUR OTHER FORMS of the verbs listed below.

    20. chew   21. eat   22. swallow

Divide each sentence into SUBJECT and PREDICATE in the usual manner and write the Pp's.

23. Omar and his friend were waiting at the foot of the cliff.

24. A man on the face of the cliff above them dangled by a rope.

25. They had been watching the fellow above them over an hour.

26. The chap on the cliff face should obviously not have attempted the climb.

27. The whole affair was becoming a lesson in patience.

28-32. Write all the MAIN VERBS and VERB CLUSTERS used above.

33-37. Write all the NOUNS used above.

Lesson 15   <u>Verbs: Derivational Suffixes</u>

Verbs are the second most common type of word in English; nouns are the first. Since **verbs are tellers** and generally represent some sort of **action**, it is easy to see that many verbs exist to describe the many and varied actions which are possible.

One manner in which verbs are created is to add a derivational suffix to another type of word. You will remember that **a derivational suffix changes the FORM and the MEANING of a word**. Verbs have FOUR BASIC DERIVATIONAL SUFFIXES which all mean *to make*, *to do*, or *to create*.

Verbs are commonly made **from nouns** by adding the suffixes *-ATE*, *-FY*, and *-ISE/IZE*.

     ☞ assassin, assassinate   ☞ beauty, beautify   ☞ energy, energize

☞ **NOTE:** In English many verbs ending in *-ATE* do not behave as the example above. 1) They add more than just the suffix or 2) do not attach to a noun recognizable as a word in English.

     ☞ adulterate, circulate   ☞ imitate, celebrate, inflate

Verbs can also be made **from a certain few adjectives** by adding the suffix *-EN*.

     ☞ sharp, sharpen

☞ **NOTE:** It is important to know that the suffixes *-EN* and *-ATE* are ALSO ADJECTIVE SUFFIXES. When the suffixes mean *to do* or *to make*, they are **verb derivational suffixes**. When they mean *having the quality of*, they are **adjective derivational suffixes**.

     ☞ wood, wooden (Adj.)   ☞ passion, passionate (Adj.)

Recognizing verbs on the basis of their derivational suffixes is not an ironclad method since **most verbs do not have derivational suffixes**. However, for those verbs which do contain a derivational suffix, it is important to determine that the suffix has the verb meaning and not an adjective meaning. Of course, all verbs except the MODALS and *BE* have the simple form and four inflected forms, so be sure to **use the test frames** or look to **see if an inflected ending <u>follows</u> the derivational ending**.

     ☞ create   Today I create.   Today he creates.   I am creating.
            makes sense, must be a Verb

     ☞ passionate   Today I passionate.   Today he passionates.   I am passionating.
            makes no sense, must not be a Verb

Verbs: Derivational Suffixes

1. List the auxiliary verb which forces an *-ING* form behind it.
2. List four modals in the past form.
3. Give the auxiliary verb which forces an *-EN* form behind it.
4. Give the form which always follows a *DO* auxiliary verb.
5. Give the ending of the third person singular verb form.
6. List any six linking verbs in simple form.
7. Give the seven other forms of *BE*.
8. List the five most common prepositions.
9. Give the three most common noun markers.
10. Give the possessive form for plurals not ending with an *S*.

Form PLURALS of the following words.

    11. penny   12. cross   13. snow

Form POSSESSIVES of the following words.

    14. man   15. men   16. Ed Stevens

Add a NOUN DERIVATIONAL SUFFIX to each of the following words.

    17. holy   18. social   19. false

Add a VERB DERIVATIONAL SUFFIX to each of the following words.

    20. familiar   21. terror   22. false

Give the FOUR OTHER FORMS for each verb listed below:

    23. begin   24. dream   25. swim

Make up SUBJECTS for the following PREDICATE: *rolled downhill.*

26. use seven words, one a possessive NM -- NM S Pp Pp

27. use five words; have a compound subject -- NM S & NM S

28. use four words, one simple subject -- NM S Pp

29. use five words, one an indefinite NM -- NM S Pp

30. use eight words, one simple subject and three NM's -- NM S Pp Pp

```
┌─────────────────────────────────────────────────────────────┐
│                        DEFINITIONS                            │
│                                                               │
│   TRANSITIVE VERB - a verb which carries the action across    │
│                from the subject to an object                  │
│   INTRANSITIVE VERB - a verb which does NOT carry action      │
│                    across to an object                        │
└─────────────────────────────────────────────────────────────┘
```

ACTION VERBS can be divided into **two different categories** depending upon their use. *TRANS* means *ACROSS*; thus, a **transitive verb carries the action across** from the subject to the object. The first noun acts upon the second noun.

> ☞ The dog chased a cat.   ☞ The boy hit the ball.

Notice how the chasing action is carried from the dog to the cat. Similarly you should see that the hitting action moves from the boy to the ball. In both of these sentences *cat* and *ball* function as objects of the action; they receive the action initiated by their respective subjects.

Some action verbs are **intransitive**. The **action is not carried across** to an object; instead the action simply happens.

> ☞ The horse walked.   ☞ The man paddled swiftly downstream at noon.

In the first example the action ends with the verb since the verb ends the sentence. In the second example you can see that the paddling action is not carried across to an object. On the other hand, added information about HOW and WHEN and WHERE the action was done is given. Note that the action is not carried to someone or something. The subject is not acting on an object; the **subject is merely acting while some additional information about the time, manner, and place of the action is given.**

Many verbs can be either transitive or intransitive; they can exist either with objects or without them. The presence of an object determines whether they are transitive or intransitive.

> ☞ The dog ate his food.   ☞ The dog ate hungrily from his dish.

The verb *ate* in the first sentence is transitive since the action of eating by the dog is operating directly on the food. ☞ **NOTE:** *food*, the object, **answers the question of what** *dog*, the subject, ate. In the second sentence the activity of eating is not carried across; nothing after the verb tells what the dog ate; thus, the verb here is intransitive.

A few verbs are always transitive; they always require an object. A few verbs are always intransitive and can not have an object. Most verbs can be either transitive or intransitive; it depends on the object being present or not.

☞ **NOTE:** Only the verb baseword or main verb is considered as transitive or intransitive. The auxiliary verbs are not distinguished as transitive or intransitive.

Transitive & Intransitive Verbs

1. Tell what must occur in a sentence for the verb to be transitive.
2. List the auxiliary verb that forces an -*EN* form behind it.
3. Give the verb form that must follow a Modal.
4. Give the verb form that must follow the auxiliary verb *DO*.
5. Give the ending for a regular verb in the -*EN* form.
6. Give the first person plural object form of the personal pronoun.
7. List any six linking verbs in simple form.
8. List any four indefinite noun markers.
9. Give the plural ending used for numbers, letters, and signs.
10. List any three verb derivational suffixes.

Form PLURALS of the following words.

    11. hutch   12. half   13. fox

Form POSSESSIVES of the following words.

    14. Merle Evans   15. student   16. rats

Give the OTHER FOUR FORMS for each verb listed below.

    17. ring   18. buy   19. fall

    20. traverse   21. go   22. fly

Divide each sentence into SUBJECT and PREDICATE in the usual manner and write the Pp's.

23. Hrothgar sensed an unusual presence in the immediate area.

24. His whole body prickled with sensations of danger and excitement.

25. Suddenly from some nearby brush a sound came softly to his ears.

26. Carefully the warrior turned his head toward the pinpointed area.

27. The tension was slowly straining his nerves to the point of cracking.

28. Write all AUXILIARY VERBS used above.

29. Write all TRANSITIVE VERBS used above.

30. Write all INTRANSITIVE VERBS used above.

Lesson 17   <u>Noun Subject & Verb Agreement</u>

Agreement between the noun subject and the verb **ALWAYS occurs between the SUBJECT and the FIRST VERB OF A VERB CLUSTER**. For verbs other than *BE*, the subject in the first or second person singular uses the simple form of the verb in the present tense. The third person singular uses the *-S* form in the present tense, and all three persons in the plural use the simple form of the verb in the present tense.

     ☞ I run; you run; he/she/it runs; we run; you run; they run.

The past tense has no variations according to subject except for *BE* forms; all other verbs use the *-ED* form.

     ☞ I ran; you ran; he/she/it ran; we ran; you ran; they ran.

The *BE* verb is a bit different. In the present tense, first person singular subjects use *AM*; second person singular subjects use *ARE*, and third person singular subjects use *IS*. All three persons in the plural present tense use *ARE*. In the past tense the first and third person singular subjects use *WAS*; second person singular and all three persons in the plural in the past tense use *WERE*. This is especially important since *BE* is often an auxiliary verb, and the first verb in a cluster is many times an auxiliary verb.

     ☞ I am; you are, he/she/it is; we are; you are; they are.
     ☞ I was; you were; he/she/it was; we were; you were; they were.

CERTAIN INDEFINITES need to be recognized as being singular even though they do not give a sense of singularity: *EACH, EVERYONE, EVERYBODY, EITHER, NEITHER, ANYBODY*, and *SOMEBODY*. As such they require the *-S* verb form, *IS*, or *WAS*.

     ☞ Each is going by himself.   ☞ Somebody calls daily.   ☞ Everybody was there.

COMPOUND SUBJECTS will give a sense of singleness or plurality. Depending on the sense, use the proper verb form. The connectors *OR* and *NOR* usually signal a singleness; *AND* usually signals plurality.

     ☞ Bacon and eggs is a good breakfast. (oneness)
     ☞ Bacon and eggs are two different commodities. (plurality)
     ☞ Either the man or his son is on the job. (singleness)

Some COLLECTIVE NOUNS may express quantity in units or as a group; again be sensitive to the sense of singleness or plurality.

     ☞ Fourteen tons was the load limit. (singleness)
     ☞ The flock on the hill is moving this way. (singleness)
     ☞ A crowd of men were all shouting at once. (plurality)

Confusion with PREPOSITIONAL PHRASES sometimes exists when a subject is followed by a noun of the opposite number before the verb occurs. Just remember that THE VERB AGREES WITH THE SUBJECT, not other nouns.

     ☞ Five bags of wheat were on the dock. (bags were)
     ☞ Milk in bottles is sold here. (milk is)

Noun Subject & Verb Agreement Exercise 17

1. List the auxiliary verb that forces an -*ING* form behind it.
2. Which verb in a verb cluster (Vcl) agrees with the subject.
3. List the verb that has two forms in the -*ED* form or simple past.
4. List the present verb form that agrees with a third person singular subject.
5. Give the present tense form of *HAVE* that agrees with subject *SHE*.
6. Give the present tense form of *BE* that agrees with the subject *I*.
7. Give the possessive ending used for plurals ending in *S*.
8. List all 12 linking verbs in their simple forms.
9. Define *SYNTAX* in two words.
10. Name the type of verb which requires an object behind it.

Form PLURALS of the following words.

      11. goat   12. clock   13. purse   14. mink

Form POSSESSIVES of the following words.

      15. Hobie Parsons   16. child   17. children   18. girls

Give the OTHER FOUR FORMS of the verbs listed below.

      19. eat   20. shovel   21. throw   22. put

Divide each sentence into SUBJECT and PREDICATE in the usual manner and write the Pp's.

23. Bill and Bob were running to the local fast food outlet.
24. Hamburgers and tacos were on special at a super cheap price.
25. About noon the whole area around the takeout windows became a madhouse.
26. Everyone was placing their lunch order at the same time.
27. A single taco or hamburger cost only thirty-five cents on sale.

28-32. Write all the NOUNS which appear and UNDERLINE the SIMPLE SUBJECTS.

33-37. Write the MAIN VERB in each sentence.

Write a sentence to fit each set of parameters below.

38. SUBJECT: 1 word, 3rd person singular subject S   PREDICATE: 4 words *BE* Vbw NM N

39. SUBJECT: 8 words NM S & NM S Pp   PREDICATE: 7 words M LV NM N Pp

40. SUBJECT: 6 words NM S Pp   PREDICATE: 6 words V & V Pp

[See Additional Exercises, pages 164-165 for more practice on Ns-V agreement.]

> **DEFINITION**
>
> **ANTECEDENT** - the word (noun) for which the pronoun stands

Pronominal nouns are those traditional **pronouns that act as nouns**. Case is the category of noun depending upon its use. **Three general cases exist in English.**

SUBJECTIVE	OBJECTIVE	POSSESSIVE
Nominative	accusative	genitive

Each case is determined by its function. The pronominal forms alter their form according to case. Lesson 9 lists the various forms for the personal pronouns. Normal nouns do not change form between the subject and object case. They do show a form change in the possessive by adding the apostrophe or apostrophe and *S*.

    ☞ dog, dog's   ☞ boys, boys'

Possessives are really no problem except for spelling errors; the key here is to see that possessive pronominals do not use an apostrophe (*ours, his, ...*). This is different from the normal nouns which do use an apostrophe.

For normal subjects and objects, most people have little problem in recognizing and using the proper pronominal forms. Three problem areas, however, are evident in normal usage.

The FIRST basic trouble spot is the SUBJECT COMPLEMENT or PREDICATE NOMINATIVE. In this case we find a linking verb and a pronominal noun referring to the subject; in fact, it completes or complements the subject. It really is just another name for the subject. As such, it **must retain the subjective case** wherein lies the problem since the objective case is used after the active verbs. Habit is our enemy here.

    ☞ That girl is she.   ☞ My friend was he.   ☞ The culprits were they.

☞ **NOTE:** A reversal of this type of sentence reveals the correctness of using the subjective forms.

    ☞ She is that girl.   ☞ He was my friend.   ☞ They were the culprits.

A SECOND trouble area is when a COMPOUND INCLUDING A PRONOMINAL is used. The **key** to correct usage here is to test which form would be **used by itself** and then use that one.

    ☞ John and I went to the store.   (I went)
    ☞ He gave it to John and me.   (to me)

A THIRD potential area of headache is when the PRONOMINAL DIRECTLY PRECEDES A NOUN. Again the **key** is to **use the pronominal** which would be used **by itself**.

    ☞ We boys went swimming yesterday.   (We went)
    ☞ The model asked us girls to hold her dresses.   (asked us)

It should be evident that the **subject form is used for the subject and the subject complement**; the **objective form is used for all objects** of which there are three: **direct**, **indirect**, and **object of the preposition**.

1. List the auxiliary verb that forces an *-EN* form behind it.
2. Which verb in a verb cluster (Vcl) agrees with the subject.
3. Give the five present tense forms of *BE*.
4. List the present verb form that agrees with a first person singular subject.
5. Give the present tense form of *HAVE* that agrees with the subject *YOU*.
6. Give the present tense form of *BE* that agrees with the subject *HE*.
7. List the two parts every prepositional phrase (Pp) must have.
8. Give the three common noun markers.
9. Give the verb which is always linking.
10. Name the type of verb which requires no object behind it.

Form PLURALS of the following words.

    11. class   12. salmon   13. bird   14. goose

Form POSSESSIVES of the following words.

    15. Frank Edwards   16. men   17. man   18. boys

Give the OTHER FOUR FORMS of the verbs listed below.

    19. purchase   20. freeze   21. shake   22. begin

Divide each sentence into SUBJECT and PREDICATE in the usual manner; write all the Pp's.

23. The elk was sneaking through the pines above the road cut.

24. On the opposite side of the hill my friend and I waited with anticipation.

25. After the sunrise we hunters had heard the bugling clearly.

26. The sounds had come to him and me from this immediate area.

27. A single noise from either side at this point would mean discovery.

28-32. Write all the NOUNS and UNDERLINE the SIMPLE SUBJECT in each list.

33-37. Write all the MAIN VERBS.

Write a sentence to fit each set of parameters below.

38. SUBJECT: 5 words   S Pp   PREDICATE: 6 words   Modal *BE* Vbw Pp

39. SUBJECT: 7 words   S & S Pp   PREDICATE: 4 words   *HAVE* LV NM N

40. SUBJECT: 1 word, 3rd person pronominal   S   PREDICATE: 6 words, 1 pronominal   V Pp Pp

Lesson 19   <u>Adjectives: Function & Position</u>

The third FORM WORD CLASS which we will discuss is the ADJECTIVE (A). Its **FUNCTION is to DESCRIBE or MODIFY a NOUN.** Actually the adjective places limits on the noun, so we can say that the adjective limits a noun. Since communication is the transferring of ideas, the more precise the transferal, the better the communication. Let's take an example. *TREE* is a noun which covers a large range of items. A more precise idea of a tree would improve the communication; adjectives will make the idea more precise by limiting the number of trees possible. Let's apply some adjectives to our tree and watch it change. Note the progressive change to a more precise and limited idea of a tree with the addition of each adjective. First think of a tree in your mind; then read each group of words and change your mind picture accordingly.

      ☞ tree   old tree   old, black tree

    old, black, dead tree   small, old, black, dead tree

         small, old, black, dead, broken tree

☞ **PUNCTUATION RULE:** When two adjectives occur side by side and modify the same noun, then they are **separated by a comma**. Such adjectives are called COORDINATE ADJECTIVES. There is a quick test to see if the comma is needed. Since the adjectives are of equal value, they can be reversed in order with no change in meaning. In that case use the comma; if the reversal does not sound right, do not use a comma.

     ☞ the big, juicy apple   the juicy, big apple   reversible order = comma

     ☞ the dark green dress   the green dark dress   non-reversible = no comma

The ADJECTIVE TEST FRAME appears below.

            He/it seems _____.

Any word that fits into the blank COULD be used as an adjective.

The position of an adjective in a sentence is determined by the noun which it modifies. Adjectives are single words. The **syntax rule of modification** states that a **SINGLE WORD modifier PRECEDES the word it modifies** while a **PHRASE modifier FOLLOWS the word it modifies.** This rule is very beneficial to know since it has much to do with punctuation of various modifiers.

In English the adjective can occupy two positions relative to the noun it modifies. The first situation follows the rule above.

        ☞ the red truck   ☞ a big dog   ☞ my juicy taco

The second situation occurs when the **adjective follows a linking verb** (LV) and relates back to the subject. This is called the PREDICATE ADJECTIVE (PA) or the ADJECTIVE SUBJECT COMPLEMENT (Asc). Please notice that in this situation the single word modifier does not precede the word it modifies.

      ☞ The truck is red.   ☞ A dog is big.   ☞ The taco seemed juicy.

Adjectives: Function & Position   Exercise 19

1. Give the function of an adjective.
2. Tell what punctuation comes between coordinate adjectives.
3. Tell where a single word modifier comes in relationship to its noun.
4. List the auxiliary verb that forces an -*ING* form behind it.
5. Give the three past tense forms of *BE*.
6. Give the present tense form of *HAVE* that agrees with the subject *IT*.
7. Give the plural ending used for most nouns.
8. Give the five forms of verbs.
9. Give the past forms of any five linking verbs.
10. Give two noun derivational suffixes which mean *ONE WHO*.

Form PLURALS of the following words.

    11. critter   12. gulf   13. witch   14. wolf

Form POSSESSIVES of the following words.

    15. Mary Smith   16. Jane Jones   17. hogs   18. pig

Give the OTHER FOUR FORMS of the verbs listed below.

    19. wear   20. place   21. teach   22. blow

Divide each sentence into SUBJECT and PREDICATE in the usual manner; write all the Pp's.

23. A beautiful chalice was the object of their search at this time.

24. Some people had spent many years in their quest for it already.

25. This small group of questors were somewhat different from the others.

26. Their elected leader and guide was an elderly man with white hair.

27. No one in our group could see any warriors among the followers.

28-32. Write all the NOUNS and UNDERLINE the SIMPLE SUBJECT in each list.

33-37. Write the MAIN VERBS in each sentence.

38. Write all of the ADJECTIVES from the above sentences.

Write a sentence to fit each set of parameters below; punctuate where necessary.

39. SUBJECT: 7 words NM A A S Pp   PREDICATE: 6 words *BE* LV A Pp

40. SUBJECT: 1 word, pronominal noun subject S   PREDICATE: 3 words M LV A

Lesson 20   Adjectives: Forms of Degree

Since the adjective is a **form word**, we need to see what inflections it has. The adjective has THREE FORMS which are generally labeled the FORMS OF DEGREE. The various forms are **used to show a differing degree of comparison**. There are **three degrees or forms**.

The FIRST form is called the **POSITIVE** or the **SIMPLE** form. It is the normal form and **has no ending**. It is the form **used when applying an adjective to a noun and making a simple statement about a quality**. It is a flat statement with no comparison made to other nouns or groups of nouns.

     ☞ The dog is black.   ☞ the big mountain   ☞ the spicy sauce
         ☞ beautiful doll   ☞ interesting book

The SECOND form is called the **COMPARATIVE** form or the *-ER* form. It is **used when comparing two items**. It either has the ending *-ER* or uses the word *MORE* or *LESS* in front of the adjective.

     ☞ My dog is blacker than your dog.   ☞ bigger mountain   ☞ spicier sauce
         ☞ more beautiful doll   ☞ less interesting book

The THIRD form of degree is called the **SUPERLATIVE** form or the *-EST* form. It is **used when the adjective is comparing one item to two or more others and setting it apart as being the most extreme example**. It ends in *-EST* or uses the word *MOST* or *LEAST* in front of the adjective.

     ☞ My dog is the blackest of all.   ☞ biggest mountain   ☞ spiciest sauce
         ☞ most beautiful doll   ☞ least interesting book

A QUICK METHOD to keep these forms straight is to know the chart below.

1 item	positive	simple
2 items	comparative	er (more/less)
3 items	superlative	est (most/least)

Deciding when to use the endings *-ER/-EST* or the words *MORE/LESS/MOST/LEAST* is rather simple. Single syllable adjectives almost always use the *-ER* or *-EST* forms and most two syllable words do likewise. Three or more syllables in the adjective require the helping words in front. A very few two syllable adjectives also use the helping words.

     ☞ 1 syllable: red, redder, reddest   slow, slower, slowest
     ☞ 2 syllables: pretty, prettier, prettiest   eager, more eager, most eager
     ☞ 3 syllables: beautiful, more beautiful, most beautiful

A few adjectives are somewhat perverse and do not follow normal methods for forming their comparative and superlative forms. They are generally well known and are listed below.

     ☞ much, more, most   ☞ little, less, least;
     ☞ good or well, better, best   ☞ bad or ill, worse, worst

Some adjectives are finite in meaning and cannot be compared: perfect, square, chief, dead, right, etc.

Never make a double comparison: more bigger, most prettiest.

Adjectives: Forms of Degree

1. List the three forms of degree of an adjective.
2. Tell which adjective form is used when comparing two items.
3. Give the form used when comparing two or more items.
4. List the auxiliary verb that forces a simple form behind it.
5. Give the eight forms of *BE*.
6. List the five most common prepositions.
7. Give the plural ending used for nouns ending in a sibilant.
8. Give the five forms of verbs.
9. Give the *-EN* forms of any five linking verbs.
10. Give one noun derivational suffix which means *LITTLE*.

Give the OTHER TWO FORMS of the ADJECTIVES listed below.

| 11. blue | 12. hostile | 13. handy | 14. terrible |

Form POSSESSIVES of the following words.

| 15. Betty Boop | 16. Jill Owens | 17. tribe | 18. clans |

Give the OTHER FOUR FORMS of the VERBS listed below.

| 19. swing | 20. bring | 21. weave | 22. keep |

Divide each sentence into SUBJECT and PREDICATE in the usual manner and write the Pp's.

23. The produce truck roared down the long ribbon of pavement.

24. The darkness of the night was no problem at this time of year.

25. In the late winter months the high desert air was crisp and clear.

26. Even a sliver of moon and a few stars shed light on the road.

27. The driver of the truck could see every bend or dip in the road under 500 yards.

28-32. Write all the NOUNS and UNDERLINE the SIMPLE SUBJECT in each list.

33-37. Write all the MAIN VERBS in the above sentences.

38. Write all the ADJECTIVES in the above sentences.

Write a sentence to fit each set of parameters below.

39. SUBJECT: 9 words NM A S Pp Pp   PREDICATE: 6 words M *BE* LV A & A

40. SUBJECT: 8 words NM S Pp Pp   PREDICATE: 5 words *HAVE* V Pp

Lesson 21   <u>Adjectives: Derivational Suffixes</u>

Adjectives generally describe or define some quality which is then applied to a noun. Adjectives are the third most numerous word class in English, and thousands of adjectives exist.

Many adjectives have been derived from nouns or verbs. This is done by adding a derivational suffix with an adjectival meaning. We will look at a few of the more common suffixes.

One suffix spelled two ways is *-ABLE/IBLE*; it is added to nouns and verbs; it means *ABLE TO (BE)*.

   ☞ (n) peace + able = peaceable   ☞ (v) adapt + able = adaptable

Many adjective suffixes have the meaning *LIKE* or *RELATED TO*. Some of these suffixes are *-AL*, *-IC*, *-INE*, *-ISH*, and of course *-LIKE*. These suffixes usually hook onto nouns. The suffix *-ANT/ENT* means the same as the others but generally associates itself with verbs.

   ☞ (n) nation + al = national   ☞ (n) angel + ic = angelic   ☞ (n) dog + like = doglike

   ☞ (n) opal + ine = opaline   ☞ (n) book + ish = bookish
   ☞ (v) defy + ant = defiant   ☞ (v) excel + ent = excellent

Many other adjective suffixes have the meaning *HAVING THE QUALITY OF*. Some of these suffixes are *-ATE*, *-FUL*, *-OUS*, *-SOME*, and *-Y*. These suffixes usually attach to both nouns and verbs.

   ☞ (n) passion + ate = passionate
   ☞ (n) shame + ful = shameful   ☞ (v) forget + ful = forgetful
   ☞ (n) danger + ous = dangerous   ☞ (v) rebel + ous = rebellious
   ☞ (n) awe + some = awesome   ☞ (v) cuddle + some = cuddlesome
   ☞ (n) art + y = arty   ☞ (v) stick + y = sticky

The suffix *-LESS* means *WITHOUT* and usually hooks to nouns.

   ☞ (n) faith + less = faithless

The suffix *-IVE* means *HAVING THE POWER OF* and normally attaches itself to verbs.

   ☞ (v) create + ive = creative

Many other adjective suffixes exist, and all have particular meanings and signify that the word is an adjective. Only the more common suffixes have been given above.

☞ **REMEMBER: An adjective can have BOTH a derivational suffix and an inflected suffix. SYNTAX will always put the inflected suffix last.**

Also, **always look at the final derivational suffix for the clue regarding word class.** If another type of derivational suffix follows an adjective suffix, the word will not be an adjective.

   ☞ excellently = adverb (ly)
   ☞ thoughtfulness = noun (ness)

1. List the three forms of degree of an adjective.
2. Give an adjective derivational suffix meaning *LIKE, RELATED TO*.
3. Give an adjective derivational suffix meaning *HAVING THE QUALITY OF*.
4. List the auxiliary verb that forces an *-ING* form behind it.
5. Give the past tense forms of *BE*.
6. Give the present tense form of *BE* that agrees with the subject *HE*.
7. Tell what must always accompany a preposition.
8. Give the three common noun markers.
9. Give the *-ING* forms of any six linking verbs.
10. Give one noun derivational suffix which means *ONE WHO*.

Give the OTHER TWO FORMS of the ADJECTIVES listed below.

     11. fat   12. white   13. sticky   14. horrible

Form POSSESSIVES of the following words.

     15. Barbara   16. Meg Lewis   17. group   18. gangs

Give the OTHER FOUR FORMS of the VERBS listed below.

     19. ring   20. sting   21. swear   22. sleep

Divide each sentence into SUBJECT and PREDICATE in the usual manner and write the Pp's.

23. Axel took the masterful sword by its functional and decorative hilt.

24. An impish aura from the pale sheen of the blade was glowing ominously.

25. Older folks from the peaceful country still spoke of the legend.

26. They believed in the magical and mysterious powers of the sword.

27. The fine sword did have a fearsome mystique about it.

28-32. Write all the NOUNS and UNDERLINE the SIMPLE SUBJECT in each list.

33. Write all of the MAIN VERBS in the above sentences.

34-38. Write/identify all of the ADJECTIVES in the above sentences.

Write a sentence to fit each set of parameters below.

39. SUBJECT: 6 words NM A A & A S PREDICATE: 6 words M *HAVE* V Pp

40. SUBJECT: 8 words NM S & NM S Pp PREDICATE: 3 words *BE* LV A

Lesson 22   Adverbs

Adverbs (B) are the last of the form words. They are the smallest class and generally the least straightforward of the form words.

Adverbs generally modify a verb in some way. They give additional information about the verb according to TIME, MANNER, or PLACE. Traditional grammar states that adverbs also modify adjectives and even other adverbs. This grammar sets those few words apart as intensifiers; they will be covered in lesson 23.

Adverbs have a peculiar characteristic in that they **are not totally bound by syntax rules**. Adverbs have the ability to move about a sentence and take up various positions without changing the meaning of the sentence. Although they cannot move just anywhere, their mobility is evident.

☞ Suddenly the boy left the table.
☞ The boy suddenly left the table.
☞ The boy left the table suddenly.

All adverbs answer one of three basic questions: WHEN, WHERE, or HOW? WHEN speaks of time; WHERE speaks of place, and HOW speaks of manner. Obviously an adverb will answer only one of the questions at a given time. Adverbs are refereed to as time, place, or manner words.

☞ The dog ran fast.   (*fast* tells how - manner)
☞ The dog ran home.   (*home* tells where - place)
☞ The dog ran yesterday.   (*yesterday* tells when - time)

From the above you will note that **sometimes a noun will function as an adverb**. When it does so, we will say that it is an adverb at that time.

☞ Yesterday was a nice day.   (*yesterday* = noun)
☞ Yesterday we went to school.   (*yesterday* = adverb)
☞ Home is a good place to be.   (*home* = noun)
☞ He ran home from the store.   (*home* = adverb)

Many adverbs are formed by adding the DERIVATIONAL SUFFIX -*LY* **to an adjective**. The adverbial -*LY* suffix means *in the manner of* and is **the common adverbial suffix**. Beware that at times the -*LY* forms an adjective instead of an adverb; this often happens when adding -*LY* **to a noun**.

☞ childishly, slowly   (B)
☞ friendly, lovely   (A)

Some but not all adverbs have forms of degree in the same manner as adjectives. Those adverbs that end in the -*LY* suffix do not show the forms of degree, but those adverbs that are words without suffixes may show the forms. The adverbs that can also be used as adjectives are the ones to show the degree forms.

☞ He ran faster than the others.   (B)
☞ He has a faster car than I.   (A)
☞ Diamond is the hardest gemstone.   (A)
☞ He looked hardest of all for the evidence.   (B)

1. List the three forms of degree for adjectives and adverbs.
2. Give an adjective derivational suffix meaning *LIKE, RELATED TO.*
3. Give the adjective derivational suffix meaning *ABLE TO (BE).*
4. Give the verb form that must follow a modal auxiliary verb.
5. Give the eight forms of *BE.*
6. Give the past tense form of *BE* that agrees with the subject *YOU.*
7. List the two past forms of verbs.
8. List three possessive noun markers.
9. Give the -*S* forms of any six linking verbs.
10. Tell which derivational suffix on a word determines its class.

Give the OTHER TWO FORMS of the ADJECTIVES listed below.

     11. passionate   12. clean   13. proper   14. ugly

Form POSSESSIVES of the following words.

     15. Alfred   16. Fern Daniels   17. girls   18. lass

Give the OTHER FOUR FORMS of the VERBS listed below.

     19. eat   20. begin   21. fix   22. flee

Divide each sentence into SUBJECT and PREDICATE in the usual manner and write the Pp's.

23. The old boat came slowly into view along the reedy shoreline.

24. The noise of the oars was a bare whisper of sound.

25. The oarsman and his companion carefully scanned the water ahead.

26. They knew the dangers of the river and their consequences.

27. The murky water rippled beneath the keel and swirled about the oars.

28-32. Write all the NOUNS and UNDERLINE the SIMPLE SUBJECT in each list.

33. Write all of the MAIN VERBS in the above sentences.

34-38. Write all of the ADJECTIVES and ADVERBS in the above and label them A or B.

Write a sentence to fit each set of parameters below.

39. SUBJECT: 9 words S Pp Pp   PREDICATE: 6 words *BE* V B Pp

40. SUBJECT: 6 words NM A S Pp   PREDICATE: 8 words *HAVE* V NM A N Pp

Intensifiers are words that limit the range of an adjective or an adverb. They **always occur with an adjective or an adverb**, never alone. Some intensifiers are shifty, however, and may be adverbs some of the time. The KEY to deciding whether they are behaving as an intensifier or a true adverb is simply to see if the suspect word is LIMITING THE WORD TO ITS IMMEDIATE RIGHT. If the word directly following the suspect word is being limited by the suspect word, then the suspect word is behaving as an intensifier. If the suspect word does not limit the word directly following it or there is no word behind it, then the suspect word is probably an adverb. SUBSTITUTION is also a good method. **Put the word VERY in place of the suspect word**. If it sounds good, the suspect word is probably an intensifier.

☞ John moved slightly.   (*slightly* = B, no word behind it)   John moved very.   NO
☞ John moved slightly forward.   (*slightly* = I, modifies *forward*)   John moved very forward.   YES
☞ John moved slightly and fell.   (*slightly* = B, doesn't modify *and*)   John moved very & fell.   NO

From the above we can see that the **intensifier always occurs directly in front of the word it limits**.
☞ **NOTE:** The word it must occur with will be either an adjective or an adverb.

> ☞ The deer ran very fast.   (*fast* = B)
> ☞ The pig is very fat.   (*fat* = A)

While an **intensifier** is not a noun modifier, it often **indirectly affects a noun since adjectives modify nouns**. For instance, think about a red truck. If we intensify the adjective with the word *VERY*, our picture of the truck is modified by the change in redness; thus, the truck is indirectly affected by the intensifier working through the adjective. Similar thoughts apply to intensifiers and verbs being limited by adverbs.

Many adjectives and adverbs can be measured or qualified on an intensity line. One end of the line is low intensity while the other end of the line is high intensity. It is the job of the intensifier to move the condition of the adjective or adverb along the intensity line to satisfy the meaning of the writer. Again think of the color red; it can range from a pinkish shade to a deep, dark red. For low intensity we might say *barely red* or *slightly red*; for middling effect we could use *rather red* or *fairly red*; for a high intensity we might say *very red* or *extremely red*.

Examples of common intensifiers appear in the box below.

VERY	RATHER	ALMOST	SOMEWHAT
SLIGHTLY	FAIRLY	BARELY	PRETTY
TREMENDOUSLY	EXTREMELY	QUITE	

Others do exist and will show up from time to time. *VERY* **is the most commonly used intensifier.** You can often but not always use it as a substitute to test if the suspect word is an intensifer. Meanings may shift, but you are looking for the right sense.

> ☞ The boy was *extraordinarily* hungry.   The boy was *very* hungry.   (Yes; it sounds good.)

It is important to know that intensifiers can be found anywhere an adjective or an adverb might be found.

> ☞ The very big dog ran very fast into the very deep water.
> ☞ The very shy girl is very nice to her very obnoxious brother.

Intensifiers Exercise 23

1. List the most common intensifier.
2. Give the two word classes an intensifier can limit.
3. Tell where an intensifier must come in relation to the word it limits.
4. Give the three questions that adverbs can answer.
5. Give the common adverbial derivational suffix.
6. Give the present tense form of *BE* that agrees with the subject *YOU*.
7. Give the possessive ending used for plural nouns ending in *S*.
8. Give an adjective derivational suffix that means *WITHOUT*.
9. Give the simple forms of any six linking verbs.
10. Give two noun derivational suffixes which mean *STATE* or *QUALITY OF*.

Give the OTHER TWO FORMS of the ADJECTIVES listed below.

    11. horrendous   12. yellow   13. tricky   14. docile

Form POSSESSIVES of the following words.

    15. Zelda   16. Slim Daws   17. elves   18. hobbit

Give the OTHER FOUR FORMS of the VERBS listed below.

    19. forgive   20. burst   21. bite   22. deal

Divide each sentence into SUBJECT and PREDICATE in the usual manner and write the Pp's.

23. The beautiful view from the uttermost top of the spire was very awesome.

24. Kearny was wondering to himself about the sheer immensity of it.

25. On his far left the dark hills of the hinterland marched to the distant plains.

26. To the right an extremely bright sea of green dominated the landscape.

27. In front of him a busy city stretched away almost forever.

28-32: Write all the NOUNS and UNDERLINE the SIMPLE SUBJECT in each list.

33. Write all the MAIN VERBS in the above sentences.

34-38. Write all ADJECTIVES, ADVERBS, and INTENSIFIERS and label them with A, B, or I.

Write a sentence to fit each set of parameters below.

39. SUBJECT: 4 words NM I A S   PREDICATE: 4 words *BE* V I B

40. SUBJECT: 7 words NM A A S Pp   PREDICATE: 5 words M *HAVE* LV I A

Formula writing is writing that follows a formula. Commonly the formula will utilize abbreviations for the various words to be used in the sentence. At times the abbreviation will reflect a WORD CLASS. At other times it may represent a FUNCTION such as subject or object, or it may stand for a GROUP OF WORDS such as a prepositional phrase. A list of common abbreviations and their meanings follow.

N	noun	NM	noun marker
V	verb (usually active)	LV	linking verb
A	adjective	I	intensifier
B	adverb	APPOS	appositive
P	preposition	Pp	prepositional phrase
S	subject (simple)	OP	object preposition
O	direct object	IO	indirect object
Asc	adjective subject complement	Nsc	noun subject complement
Vbw	main verb or verb base word	Nbw	noun base word
	M	modal: *can, could, will...*		
	HAVE	a form of *HAVE* as an auxiliary verb		
	BE	a form of *BE* as an auxiliary verb		
	c/c	coordinating conjunction: the FANBOYS *for, and....*		

Punctuation may be included or left up to you. Some of the abbreviations in the above list have already been discussed; you will learn the others later as well as a few more.

You have been doing a little of this already. Look at the formula given below.

$$NM \ A \ N \ Pp \ V \ NM \ A \ N \ Pp.$$

Your job would be to write a sentence which conforms to the formula. You should note immediately that the verb is active. **The type of verb determines** to a large degree **the type of sentence** that can be written. It is easiest to **pick a subject and verb first and build on the rest**.

☞ boy // eats   N -- V

Now you can **build up the subject** since you know it is a boy.

☞ the big boy in the car   NM A N Pp = subject

Next, look at the predicate. This requires a bit more care than the subject due to the choice of the verb. **After the verbs another word in the predicate is often important. Try to identify that word and fill it in. Try the nouns first.** When no noun appears, an adjective might be the main item if the verb is linking.

☞ eats tacos   V -- N

Now you can flesh out the rest of the predicate.

☞ eats his favorite tacos with mustard   V NM A N Pp = predicate

THUS: The big boy in the car eats his favorite tacos with mustard.

Formula Writing

1. List the nine modals.
2. Tell which word class has endings such as -*MENT* and -*NESS*.
3. Give the three common noun markers.
4. Give the verb which is always linking.
5. List the three questions adverbs answer.

Give the PLURALS of the following nouns.

    6. 100   7. steelhead   8. woman   9. ox

Form POSSESSIVES of the following words.

    10. Don and Jay   11. Inky Shmoo   12. dart   13. Bess

Give the OTHER TWO FORMS of the ADJECTIVES listed below.

    14. yellow   15. goofy   16. courteous   17. bad

Give the OTHER FOUR FORMS of the VERBS listed below.

    18. rise   19. fly   20. chomp   21. know

Divide each sentence into SUBJECT and PREDICATE in the usual manner and write the Pp's.

22. The diligent student labored thoughtfully over his last assignment.

23. Some of the very difficult problems required extreme concentration.

24. From the corner of his eye he noticed a slip of yellow paper.

25. It was a note from his friend in the math class of the previous period.

26. Rather quickly the student diverted his attention back to his work.

27-31. Write the BASIC FORMULA for each sentence above; punctuate if needed.

Write sentences to fit the formulas below.

32. NM A N Pp M *BE* V NM N.

33. Pp NM N Pp *BE* V NM I A N.

34. NM A N P NM A OP V B.

35. NM I A N Pp *HAVE* V NM N c/c NM N Pp.

Lesson 25 Internal Punctuation 1

Internal punctuation refers to the use of commas within a simple sentence. Major punctuation refers to the punctuation between simple sentences that are placed together into one sentence.

The comma is the common element used in internal punctuation. There are a few basic situations or rules for internal punctuation. This lesson will review three of them.

The FIRST situation is DIRECT ADDRESS. Direct address is when the name or some definite reference of someone is used in a sentence, and the sentence is directed at that person. No matter where the name is stated in the sentence, it is set off by commas. In practice the noun of direct address usually comes first or last, but it may come somewhere in the middle as well.

> ☞ John, let's go to town.
> ☞ Is the kitchen clean yet, Audrey?
> ☞ It is time, my friend, to lock the door.

The SECOND rule involves FOUR BASIC WORDS: *YES, NO, WELL,* and *OH*. When any of these words is used as the **first word in a sentence**, they are to be set off by a comma. EXCLAMATORY WORDS such as *WOW, WHY,* or *GOOD GRIEF* are also set off from the rest of the sentence with a comma if they are not followed by an exclamation mark.

> ☞ Yes, we will go to town.
> ☞ Why, he certainly surprised me.
> ☞ Well, it should be a winner.

A THIRD comma rule involves a SERIES. A series is a group of words all of the same type, most normally nouns or phrases. Each element in the series is of equal value grammatically to the other elements. A series consists of at least three elements; the final element is often connected to the rest of the series by the words *AND* or *OR*. The comma between the final element is optional if either of the connecting words occurs and the meaning is clear without the comma.

> ☞ He ate lettuce, tomatoes, and potato chips.
> ☞ The dog ran, jumped and barked.
> ☞ Our government is of the people, by the people, and for the people.

A note on usage should be emphasized here. **Each element in the series is to be grammatically equal.** Unequal items do not fit together in a series.

> ☞ He wanted dinner, dessert and to take a nap.

The first two items are nouns while the third element is a phrase; the items are not equal grammatically and should not be together in a series. The above sentence should be rewritten as given below.

> ☞ He wanted dinner, dessert, and a nap.

1. List the five most common prepositions.
2. Give the common intensifier.
3. Give the common adverbial derivational suffix.
4. Give the term that means *WORD ORDER*.
5. Give the minimum number of grammatically equal elements necessary for a series.

Give the PLURALS of the following nouns.

    6. dog   7. sheep   8. man   9. mouse

Give the POSSESSIVE of the following words.

    10. Ed and Bill   11. Dan Foss   12. people   13. nations

Give the OTHER TWO FORMS of the ADJECTIVES listed below.

    14. red   15. polite   16. gracious   17. angry

Give the OTHER FOUR FORMS of the VERBS listed below.

    18. rush   19. weep   20. bring   21. choose

Divide each sentence into SUBJECT and PREDICATE in the usual manner and write the Pp's.

22. It was a beautiful day in the early morning mists of the mountains.

23. Squirrels birds and other creatures were loudly making their morning noises.

24. In a small glade a young doe was quietly munching grass and keeping a lookout.

25. A cottontail in the shadow of a berry patch was sniffing the air.

26. Yes the day was beginning with much of Gods glory in evidence.

27-31. Write the basic FORMULA for each sentence; punctuate if needed.

Write sentences to fit the parameters below; punctuate if necessary.

32. S Pp Pp M LV Asc.

33. S S c/c S Pp *BE* V V c/c V Pp.

34. S V B Pp.

35. NM I A S Pp *BE* V NM A N Pp.

```
                        DEFINITION
    OBJECT (O) - the receiver of the action (direct object)
```

You will remember that most nouns can do any of six various jobs in a sentence. We have previously looked at nouns as modifiers, nouns as subjects, and nouns as objects of prepositions.

The object of a sentence occurs only if a certain type of verb is present; it is a TRANSITIVE VERB (see Lesson 15). **The object receives the action** of the transitive verb.

The action in a sentence flows through the sentence; it begins with the subject or doer of the action; it moves to the verb which tells what action is being done, and it ends with the object which is acted upon. Visualize a line in the sentence which we will call the movement line. The line begins with the subject and moves in a direct line through the verb to the object. The line is a graphic representation of how the action moves in a sentence.

$$S \rightarrow V \rightarrow O$$

☞ The hunter shot the bear.

In the sentence above, *HUNTER* is the **subject or doer of the action**; the hunter initiates the action. The verb *SHOT* **tells us what action is taking place**. *BEAR* **is the object, the recipient of that action**.

An easy way **to find the direct object of any sentence** is to say the subject and verb along with the question WHAT? For the above sentence we would say, "The hunter shot what?" The obvious answer is *BEAR*, which in this sentence is the object.

There are instances where there is more than one simple object in a sentence. This occurs when two or more nouns are connected by the coordinating conjunctions *AND* or *OR*. Two nouns sharing the object position are called compound objects.

☞ Henry ate tacos and tamales for lunch.

Both *TACOS* and *TAMALES* are objects in the example sentence since they are equally yoked with the word *AND*. They are an example of a compound object.

☞ **NOTE:** It is important to note that while subjects can occur with all types of verbs, **objects require an active transitive verb**. Linking verbs or intransitive verbs will **not** have objects following them.

The **symbols** used in this text to designate various objects follow:

$$
\begin{array}{lll}
O & = & \text{direct object} \\
IO & = & \text{indirect object} \\
OP & = & \text{object of the preposition}
\end{array}
$$

Noun Functions 2 Exercise 26

Form PLURALS of the following NOUNS.

  1. tomato   2. dwarf   3. candle   4. louse

Give the OTHER FOUR FORMS of the VERBS listed below.

  5. run   6. help   7. steal   8. keep

  9. For each of the following, divide into SUBJECT and PREDICATE in the usual manner.

A. The old owl watched silently from his perch.

B. The mouse in the grass was oblivious to the threat.

C. He was seeking ripe grain or fruit for food.

D. The hungry mouse ran eagerly across the field.

E. Very suddenly on soft wings the owl struck from the sky.

10-14. Write the NOUNS, MAIN VERBS, and Pp's in each sentence.

15. Write all the DIRECT OBJECTS from the above sentences.

Write a sentence for each of the formulas below. Tie all five of the sentences together in context so that they form a story or description.

16. S V O Pp.

17. Pp S V B Pp.

18. S Pp V Pp O Pp.

19. S Pp V O & O Pp.

20. Pp NM A N M V O Pp Pp.

```
┌─────────────────────────────────────────────────────────────┐
│                          DEFINITION                           │
│   INDIRECT OBJECT (IO) - the receiver of the direct object    │
└─────────────────────────────────────────────────────────────┘
```

Last lesson we learned of the direct object. In this lesson we will find another object. Like the direct object, the **indirect object must occur with a transitive verb;** however, the indirect object **occurs only with a limited number** of transitive verbs.

Some verbs of this type are *GIVE*, *BUY*, *SEND*, *TAKE*, and *BRING*. It is important to note that **these verbs do not automatically have an indirect object**; it merely means that this type of verb is necessary for an indirect object to occur.

Also, **there must always be a direct object for an indirect object to occur**. The indirect object is the recipient of the object. The movement line in this type of sentence begins with the subject or doer of the action; it moves to the verb which tells what action is being done; it then goes to the object of the sentence; finally it returns back to indirect object. The **indirect object comes between the verb and object.**

☞ John gave his mother some flowers.

First let us find the object. We do this by saying the subject and verb and *WHAT*. "John gave what?" It is obvious that John did not give his mother; rather he did give some flowers. Thus we see that *FLOWERS* is the direct object. Now **to find the indirect object we ask another question**, "WHO or WHAT RECEIVED the flowers?" The answer is that his mother received the flowers; this means *MOTHER* is the indirect object.

In the sentence above, *JOHN* is the subject or doer of the action; John initiates the action. The verb *GAVE* tells us what action is taking place. *FLOWERS* is the object, the recipient of that action. *MOTHER* is the indirect object since she receives the flowers.

There are instances where there is more than one indirect object in a sentence. This occurs when two or more nouns are connected by the coordinating conjunctions *AND* or *OR*. Two nouns sharing the indirect object position are called compound indirect objects.

☞ John gave his mother and sister a present.

Both *MOTHER* and *SISTER* are indirect objects in the example sentence since they are equally yoked with the word *AND*. They are an example of a compound indirect object.

It is important to note that the indirect object can be rewritten as an object of a preposition.

☞ The man gave the girl a rose.
☞ The man gave a rose to the girl.

In the first sentence *GIRL* is an indirect object; in the second, *GIRL* is the object of the preposition *TO*.

Form POSSESSIVES of the following NOUNS.

1. boy   2. boys   3. Joe & Ed   4. Amos

Give the OTHER TWO FORMS of the ADJECTIVES listed below.

5. bright   6. dandy   7. odious   8. good

9. Divide each sentence into SUBJECT and PREDICATE in the usual manner.

A. The friendly boy in the first row smiled at the girl beside him.

B. The girl was wearing a blue skirt and a pink blouse.

C. She handled his attentions with grace and charm.

D. The boy reached into his coat pocket for a moment.

E. Then he gave the girl a note with a poem and flowers on it.

10-14: Write the NOUNS, MAIN VERBS, and Pp's in each sentence.

15. Write all the DIRECT OBJECTS from the above sentences.

Write a sentence to fit each set of parameters below. Tie all five of the sentences together in context so that they form a story or description.

16. S V B Pp.

17. Pp S V O Pp.

18. S Pp V Pp O Pp.

19. S Pp V O & O Pp.

20. Pp S V IO O Pp.

DEFINITION
NOUN SUBJECT COMPLEMENT (Nsc)- complements the subject, it is a
second name for the subject but found in the predicate

In this lesson we will learn of yet another function of the noun. This function is called the **noun subject complement (Nsc) or the predicate nominative (PN).** Either name is correct; they can be used interchangeably. **The Nsc or PN is a noun that equals the subject; it is another name for the subject.**

The Nsc or PN must come after a linking verb. There are **only three linking verbs** (LV) that are **commonly used**: *BE, BECOME,* and *REMAIN.* These verbs do not automatically have a Nsc following them; it merely means that these verbs are necessary for a Nsc to occur.

> ☞ The man is my friend.
> ☞ The dog became a good hunter.

☛ **NOTE:** *MAN* and *FRIEND* are the same person; *DOG* and *HUNTER* equal one another. The subject and noun subject complement are the same entity.

On rare occasions certain other verbs can be found between the subject and the noun subject complement. In each case the verb will be used in the sense of *BE, BECOME,* or *REMAIN.*

> ☞ The man turned traitor.

In this case, the word *TURNED* is used in the sense of the word *BECAME.*

The movement line in this type of sentence begins at the equality verb points both ways, to the subject and to the noun subject complement. The S and the Nsc are equal; they name the same noun and are simply linked together with an equality verb. There is no action, just an equality.

S　←　LV　→　Nsc

In the sentence above, *MAN* is the subject; the verb *IS* tells us that an equality is being stated. *TRAITOR* is the Nsc since it equals *MAN.*

There are instances where there is more than one Nsc in a sentence. This occurs when two or more nouns are connected by the coordinating conjunctions *AND* or *OR.* Two nouns sharing the Nsc position are called **compound noun subject complements**.

> ☞ The boy is my friend and cousin.

Both FRIEND and COUSIN are Nsc's in the example sentence since they are equally yoked with the word *AND.* They are an example of a compound noun subject complement.

It is important to know that the case of the Nsc or PN is the subjective or nominative case. This determines our choice of personal pronouns used in the Nsc position.

> ☞ My friend is she.　　It was I.

Form PLURALS of the following NOUNS.

    1. troop   2. fox   3. bath   4. child

Give the OTHER FOUR FORMS of the following VERBS.

    5. check   6. break   7. slide   8. ring

9. For each of the following, divide into SUBJECT and PREDICATE in the usual manner.

A. Folmar wielded his mace with deftness and accuracy.

B. The brigand to his immediate right was the target.

C. A direct hit on the leather shield might break or injure his arm.

D. At the very least it would be an advantage for Folmar.

E. The blow from the mace was a smashing success at first contact.

10-14. Write the NOUNS, MAIN VERBS, and Pp's in each sentence; punctuate if needed.

15. Write all the NOUN SUBJECT COMPLEMENTS from the above sentences.

Write a sentence for each of the formulas below. Tie all five of the sentences together in context so that they form a story or description.

16. S V B Pp.

17. Pp S LV Nsc Pp.

18. S Pp V Pp O Pp.

19. S Pp Pp V O Pp.

20. Pp S V O Pp.

Lesson 29 Looking to the Left

Since the noun has various functions which it can play in a sentence, it would be nice to have a handy method of determining the specific function of a noun in any given situation. Fortunately, such a system exists due the syntax of English. You will remember that English is a syntactical language, a language where words take on meaning relative to other words in their sentence. Consider the two sentences given below.

☞ The dog bit the man.   ☞ The man bit the dog.

In the first sentence *DOG* is the subject and is doing the biting while *MAN* is receiving the action and is therefore the object. In the second sentence the roles are reversed. Note that the forms of the words did not change; only their relative positions in the sentence shifted. The word order or syntax determines the function of the two nouns in each sentence, and the function of the nouns determines to some degree the meaning of the sentence.

Thus, knowing the function of a noun in a sentence is helpful when describing the sentence and determining its exact meaning. Finding out what the function of a given noun is in any situation is accomplished in most cases by looking to the left and checking the syntax.

The key to the system is to find the noun in question and look to its immediate left. There are two types of key words to look for: prepositions and verbs. The key words will be near by, generally not more than three or four words to the left; in fact, at times the key word will be the immediate leftward word. The method described below is a process of elimination and is based on frequency of usage.

    1) locate the noun in question
    2) look to the left
        a) if a **preposition** is found, function = **OP**
        b) if an **active verb** is found, function** = **O**
        c) if a **linking verb** is found, function = **SC (Nsc)**
    d) if **none of the above** is found, probable function = **S**

NOTE 1 - Under normal conditions at least one subject is necessary in each sentence.
NOTE 2 - Subjects occur to the left of main verbs.
NOTE 3 - Appositives have the same case/function as the noun they follow (see Lesson 36)

    e) two other noun functions exist
        1) MOD: points to another noun directly to its **right**
        2) ** IO: a *GIVE* type verb on the left and a noun on the right

Observe the process in action in the following sentence. All nouns are identified for ease of instruction.

☞ The old *man* from the *country* observed the *crowd* with a *feeling* of *dread*.

Looking to the left of *COUNTRY, FEELING*, and *DREAD*, prepositions are found; hence, the three words are all OP's. Looking to the left of *MAN*, no preposition or verb is found; it must be the subject. Looking to the left of *CROWD*, an active verb is found; thus, *CROWD* is the direct object of the verb.

Looking to the Left

Form POSSESSIVES of the following NOUNS.

1. child   2. children   3. cats   4. Sam

Give the OTHER FOUR FORMS of the VERBS listed below.

5. bloat   6. find   7. trail   8. catch

9. For each of the following, divide into SUBJECT and PREDICATE in the usual manner.

A. The young wrangler was making his way around the herd at night.

B. A big steer suddenly stood up and looked off into the darkness.

C. The cowboy stopped his horse and listened for any hint of danger.

D. Somewhere to his left the darkness was a place of some unseen activity.

E. The sudden snap of a twig in the darkness gave him a jolt of fear.

10-14. Write the NOUNS, MAIN VERBS, and Pp's in each sentence; punctuate if needed.

15-19. Write the FUNCTION of each noun from the above sentences.

Write a sentence to fit each set of parameters below. Tie all five of the sentences together in context so that they form a story or description.

20. Pp S V O Pp.

21. Pp S LV Nsc Pp.

22. S V Pp Pp.

23. S Pp LV Nsc.

24. Pp Pp S V O c/c O Pp.

[See Additional Exercises, pages 166-168 for more practice on noun functions.]

Lesson 30 Adjective Subject Complement

> **DEFINITION**
> **ADJECTIVE SUBJECT COMPLEMENT (Asc)** - complements the subject;
> it describes the subject but is found in the predicate

This lesson deals with an adjective function. This function is called **the adjective subject complement (Asc) or the predicate adjective (PA).** Either name is correct; they can be used interchangeably. **The Asc or PA is an adjective in the predicate that refers back to the subject.**

The Asc or PA must come after a linking verb. All linking verbs (LV) can have an Asc follow them. These verbs do not automatically have an Asc following them; it merely means that the linking verb is necessary for an Asc to occur.

> ☞ The man is nice.
> ☞ The dog seems happy.

Note that *MAN* and *DOG* are being talked about by the predicate adjectives *NICE* and *HAPPY*.

Only one of the linking verbs, *SEEM*, can be counted on to have a PA following it. All the other LV's can have nouns or adverbs following them.

> ☞ The dog smells good.   (PA/Asc)
> ☞ The dog smells well.   (B - tells **how** his nose works)
> ☞ The dog is happy.   (PA/Asc)
> ☞ The dog is a mutt.   (PN/Nsc)

If *SEEM* is followed by the word *TO* and a verb, the resulting infinitive construction will still describe the subject of the sentence and will be used in the sense of an adjective.

> ☞ The dog seems to be chasing a rainbow.

There are instances where there is more than one PA/Asc in a sentence. This occurs when two or more adjectives are connected by the coordinating conjunctions *AND* or *OR*. Two adjectives sharing the PA/Asc position are called **compound predicate adjectives**.

> ☞ The boy is strong and handsome.

Both *STRONG* and *HANDSOME* are PA/Asc's in the example sentence since they are equally yoked with the word *AND*. They are an example of a **compound adjective subject complement**.

The movement line in this type of sentence begins with the adjective subject complement; it moves backward through the linking verb to the subject. The sentence is circular in the sense that it begins and ends with the focus on the subject.

S ← LV ← Asc

Form POSSESSIVES of the following NOUNS.

  1. man   2. men   3. Agness   4. kids

Give the OTHER FOUR FORMS of the following VERBS.

  5. write   6. treat   7. build   8. bring

  9. For each of the following, divide into SUBJECT and PREDICATE in the usual manner.

  A. Alamak was feeling somewhat funny about the recent event.

  B. The pie salesman had allowed him a taste of a new product.

  C. The frothy icing seemed very gooey and sticky at first.

  D. Then quite suddenly the icing tickled Alamaks nose.

  E. The resultant sneeze was beautiful but with messy results.

10-14: Write the NOUNS, MAIN VERBS (identify type V or LV), and Pp's in each sentence; punctuate if needed.

15. Write all the PREDICATE ADJECTIVES from the above sentences.

Write a sentence for each of the formulas below. Tie all five of the sentences together in context so that they form a story or description.

16. S V B Pp.

17. Pp S LV Asc Pp.

18. S V O Pp.

19. S Pp LV Asc & Asc.

20. Pp S V Pp.

A basic sentence is a sentence that is simple, declarative, and in the active voice. It is not a compound sentence or a complex sentence; it has only one complete thought with one subject and one predicate. It is not a question or a command but rather makes a simple statement. It is not passive or transformed from the natural subject and predicate order.

Basic sentences fall into **two basic categories**, those with active verbs and those with linking verbs. This book will divide the basic sentences into **five basic types**; these five types will include most of the sentences seen in English. Below is a list of the five types.

1. S V (B)	One patterns quickly.	
2. S V O	Two has an object.	
3. S LV N	Three is a noun.	(Nsc/PN)
4. S LV A	Four seems descriptive.	(Asc/PA)
5. S V IO O	Five gives the pattern another object.	

You will notice some things about the five patterns. First, the sentence that follows each is an example of that pattern. Second, only patterns 3 and 4 have linking verbs. Third, you will notice that the adverb in pattern 1 has parentheses around it; this means it may or may not occur, that is, being there does not affect the pattern. B stands for adverbs or Pp's used as adverbs.

It is evident that all five patterns have subjects. They also all have a verb, but the verb is where the differences begin to occur. From this we can see that **it is important to be able to recognize verbs when we see them; it is also important to be able to determine whether a verb is active or linking.** The easiest way to decide if a verb is active or linking is simply to memorize the twelve or so linking verbs and their forms. If the suspect verb matches a verb in the linking list, it is probably linking. If not, then it is generally active. **Recognizing the verb type is critical in determining the proper pattern.**

On the supplemental chart at the front of the book, the **Basic Sentence Patterns Information Sheet**, the actual process for determining pattern type is outlined.

Discerning pattern types is somewhat helpful, but being able to write the various kinds of patterns and knowing their particular uses is invaluable for improving writing skills. Mastering basic patterns and expanding them through modification and addition allows for greater flexibility in writing style. That is, or at least should be, our major goal in learning grammar.

Notice that the movement of each sentence is somewhat different. Obviously patterns 3 and 4 stress the subject while pattern 1 stresses the verb. Patterns 2 and 5 put emphasis on the nouns behind the verb. Each pattern is thus suited to do a particular job better than the other patterns. Using the correct pattern for the job desired improves the communication.

A note on the formulas: S LV N = S LV Nsc; S LV A = S LV Asc; the LV makes the N or A an SC. You will find it both ways in this book; either is correct.

Basic Sentence Patterns Exercise 31

Form POSSESSIVES of the following NOUNS.

    1. boy   2. boys   3. Bill & Jim   4. women

Give the OTHER FOUR FORMS of the VERBS listed below.

    5. try   6. blow   7. wear   8. spin

9-13. For each sentence below do the following:
    a) Divide each sentence into SUBJECT and PREDICATE in the usual manner.
    b) Write all Pp's.
    c) Write S along with the simple subject.
    d) Write V or LV along with the Vbw's.
    e) Give the basic pattern of the sentence.

9. Fiodor was searching the rubble in one corner of the room.

10. The others in his outfit were keeping a close watch on the door.

11. A sense of unrest and caution was second nature with this crew.

12. Suddenly one fellow gave the others a signal of warning.

13. Silently the brigands drifted toward the shadows near the archway.

Write sentences which fit the formulas below; tie them together into a single story or description.

14. S V B.

15. S V O Pp.

16. S LV Nsc

17. S Pp LV Asc

18. S V IO O Pp

[See Additional Exercises, pages 169-173 for more practice with basic sentence patterns.]

Lesson 32   <u>Prepositional Phrase Placement</u>

The prepositional phrase (Pp) is probably the most commonly encountered construction in English. Pp's seem to occur everywhere in all kinds of sentences. They are easy to use and quite familiar. In fact, they are often used by many people to an extreme.

The **placement of the Pp's is really quite regulated and identifiable when the syntax of a sentence is examined.** We will look at the various positions and illustrate them with examples.

Being able to recognize Pp's will help a great deal when seeking the basic pattern of a sentence. **Pp's are modifiers** and are therefore **disposable**. Some meaning will be lost, but the kernel sentence will still be in place.

Pp's can begin sentences. When a Pp starts a sentence, it can modify the entire sentence, or it can refer to just the subject of the sentence.

> ☞ At the dawning we will eat breakfast.
> ☞ In his frustration the boy tore up his paper.

The first example shows sentence modification; the second example shows modification of the subject. Often two or three Pp's can be strung together. They will act as a unit and either modify the entire sentence or the subject.

> ☞ At the crack of dawn the first hunter appeared on the horizon.

When a Pp or group of Pp's begins a sentence, there may be a need for punctuation. The criteria to use is the number of words present. If the Pp construction is four words or less, then no punctuation is necessary unless a clarity problem exists. **If the Pp construction is six words or more, a comma is needed.** Some five word constructions also need punctuation. In this book we will stick with six words as the limit.

> ☞ From the start of the story to its end, we were all expectant.

Pp's usually follow the word they modify. In most cases the word will be a noun of some importance in the sentence; otherwise it is a verb. In that case the Pp will probably be adverbial in nature.

> ☞ The man from the hill country is a good trapper.
> ☞ He caught the bear by the foot.
> ☞ The bear stepped into the trap.

NOTE: Pp's that follow the words they modify rarely have any punctuation separating them from the rest of the sentence.

Here are schematics to show where Pp's generally go in basic sentence patterns.

Pp S Pp V Pp.
Pp S Pp V Pp O Pp.
Pp S Pp LV Asc Pp.
Pp S Pp LV Nsc Pp.
Pp S Pp V Pp IO Pp O Pp.

Form POSSESSIVES of the following NOUNS.

   1. Sam   2. Bess   3. Hank & Joe   4. dogs

Give the OTHER FOUR FORMS of the following VERBS.

   5. fight   6. bend   7. crack   8. take

9-13. For each sentence below do the following:
   a) Divide each sentence into SUBJECT and PREDICATE in the usual manner.
   b) Write all Pp's.
   c) Write S along with the simple subjects and V or LV with the Vbw's.
   d) Give the basic pattern of the sentence.
   e) Punctuate if needed.

  9. Esteban and his friends were running toward the water near the bay.

10. In the early morning light a vague form was appearing from the fog.

11. Each of the boys was young and eager for the adventure.

12. Through the mist and fog on the sea a dark form emerged.

13. It was their fathers ship at the mouth of the bay.

Write sentences which fit the formulas below; tie them together into a single story or description.

14. Pp S V B Pp.

15. S Pp Pp V O Pp.

16. S LV Nsc Pp.

17. Pp S Pp LV Asc Pp.

18. S V IO Pp O Pp.

A noun cluster (Ncl) is the group of words that form around a noun baseword (Nbw). Those words which precede the Nbw will be our major concern in this lesson.

The words which precede the Nbw rarely change their order. They may or may not occur, but they almost always occur in the order given below.

☞ NM I A I B V N Nbw

☞ **NOTE:** In any given Ncl, any combination of the noun modifiers may or may not be present. The intensifier (I) will only occur when the adjective (A) or adverb (B) is present since the intensifier modifies the A or B instead of the Nbw directly.

NM A V Nbw	the old racing horse
NM V N Nbw	the racing stable horse
A N Nbw	old stable horse
NM I A V Nbw	the very old racing horse
I A V Nbw	very old racing horse
A Nbw	old horse
B V Nbw	quickly running horse
I B V Nbw	very quickly running horse

The adjective (A) is the only noun modifier that occurs more than once in the Ncl. When two or more A's occur, they are coordinate adjectives and require punctuation, commas, or the use of the word *and*.

NM A A A Nbw	the large, angry, black bear
NM A A V Nbw	the young, beautiful prancing horse

The Ncl can be found anywhere the Nbw can occur. The Ncl does not change the pattern of a sentence. The basic positions of Ncl's are subject, object, indirect object, noun subject complement, and at times the object of a preposition.

S	Bats fly.	Most very large bats fly.
O	John eats tacos.	John eats the biggest, juiciest tacos.
SC	She is a nurse.	She is a rather effective nurse.
IO	He gave the girl a ring.	He gave the happily smiling girl a ring.
OP	The boy is in town.	The boy is in a very small mining town.

Noun Cluster Structure

Form the POSSESSIVES of the following NOUNS.

   1. Flora   2. nags   3. border   4. Fess

Give the FOUR OTHER FORMS of the VERBS listed below.

   5. leap   6. pour   7. sell   8. eat

9-13. For each sentence below do the following:
  a) Divide each sentence into SUBJECT and PREDICATE in the usual manner.
  b) Write all Pp's.
  c) Write S along with the simple subjects and V or LV with the Vbw's.
  d) Give the basic pattern of the sentence.
  e) Punctuate if needed.

  9. A small and agile moth was fluttering in the corner of the room.

10. It was very early morning in the old woodcutters cottage by the river.

11. The black searching cat peered up at the small hovering moth.

12. From the back of the cottage through the curtain some sounds issued forth.

13. The ancient yet hardy woodcutter was washing his face in the basin in the next room.

Write sentences which fit the formulas below; tie them together into a single story or description.

14. S V O Pp.

15. S Pp V O Pp.

16. S LV Asc Pp.

17. S Pp V O Pp & Pp.

18. S V Pp O Pp.

This lesson in punctuation will cover **dates, addresses,** and **clarity.**

Commas are commonly used to **set off elements in dates and addresses.**

☞ We went to town on Wednesday, June 15, 1988.
☞ She lives at 419 Baker Street, Selma, Oregon.
☞ Sam's address is 523 Queens Avenue, Wolf Creek, OR 97538.

☛ **NOTE:** The **zip code** in an address is **not set off** from the rest of the address by a comma.

Variations on the rules do occur if certain conditions are met. For instance, if a date consists only of the month and year, it is not necessary to use commas.

☞ We went to the Grand Canyon in April 1983.

Similarly if prepositions are used between elements of a date or an address, punctuation is not necessary.

☞ We saw him last on April 14 in 1975.
☞ He lives at 437 Coburg Road near Eugene in Oregon.

☛ **NOTE:** When the year in a complete date has more sentence following it, a comma follows the date.

☞ On December 15, 1967, we bought our first car.

We have aforementioned the need to punctuate introductory prepositional phrases if they are six words or more. At times the need to punctuate shorter phrases occurs when there is a clarity problem. The clarity question arises when the sentence could be read two possible ways without a comma.

☞ In the morning light filtered through the trees.
☞ On the radio programs are either exciting or dull.

☛ **NOTE:** A quick reading of the sentences above is confusing at first until we go back and look for another meaning. A comma between *MORNING* and *LIGHT* and between *RADIO* and *PROGRAMS* would make the sentence clearer and thus more readily readable. The goal of good writing in clear communication, so we should attempt to write sentences which are clear to the reader.

☞ In the morning, light filtered through the trees.
☞ On the radio, programs are either exciting or dull.

Internal Punctuation 2 **Exercise 34**

Form POSSESSIVES of the following NOUNS.

   1. Sally   2. Jill Moss   3. family   4. bride

Give the OTHER FOUR FORMS of the following VERBS.

   5. jump   6. weave   7. get   8. come

9-13.   For each sentence below do the following:
    a) Divide each sentence into SUBJECT and PREDICATE in the usual manner.
    b) Write all Pp's.
    c) Write S along with the simple subjects and V or LV with the Vbw's.
    d) Give the basic pattern of the sentence.
    e) Punctuate if needed.

  9. A sleek black cat near the fireplace opened his yellow eyes.

10. At the far side of the room a small noise attracted her attention.

11. Instantaneously but quietly she perked up her ears and waited.

12. From the back of a stack of papers a rustling sound emanated again.

13. It was the sound of a mouse moving along some papers by the wall.

For each of the sentences below supply the needed punctuation.

14. Fred let's go to your brothers house.

15. He lives at 1197 East Brookside Appleton Wisconsin.

Write sentences which fit the formulas below; tie them together into a single story or description. Use subjects that contain more than two words.

16. S LV Asc Pp.

17. S Pp V O Pp.

18. S LV Nsc Pp.

19. Pp S V O Pp.

20. S V Pp Pp.

Lesson 35　　Usage: Lie/Lay, Sit/Set, Rise/Raise

Correct usage of certain elements in the English language is something that must be learned and practiced for most of us. Since we learn our language from our parents and a few other close associates, we tend to copy their usage patterns. If we are fortunate, our parents use the correct words in their speech. In that case we simply learn what is correct. Too often, however, incorrect usage in one area or another is the case, hence this lesson.

The three sets of words in the lesson title are often confused. Seeing the pattern of these words should help you with their correct use. The first verb of each set is intransitive; it takes no object. The second verb of each set is transitive and needs an object. Below those on the left are intransitive while those on the right are transitive.

INTRANSITIVE			TRANSITIVE		
lie	sit	rise	lay	set	raise
lies	sits	rises	lays	sets	raises
lying	sitting	rising	laying	setting	raising
lay	sat	rose	laid	set	raised
lain	sat	risen	laid	set	raised

The simple way to use these words correctly is to use a substitute word to check the sense of the sentence. Using a form of the word *PLACE* will let you know whether the transitive form fits or not. If *PLACE* or a form of it fits in the sentence, it means the sentence has an object and needs the transitive form.

☞　The dog is (lying/laying) on the rug.

Trial:　The dog is (placing) on the rug. (sounds poor, intransitive)
Thus:　The dog is lying on the rug.

☞　The explosion (rose/raised) the roof.

Trial:　The explosion (placed) the roof. (sounds OK, transitive)
Thus:　The explosion raised the roof.

A very slight problem emerges in that the simple form of *LAY* is also the past form of *LIE*. In that particular case, recognizing the tense of the sentence will give us the hint as to the correct form to use.

☞　The paper (lay/laid) on the step.

Tense tells us it is past since the forms are -ED forms.
Trial:　The paper (placed) on the step. (sounds poor, intransitive)
Thus:　The paper lay on the step.

☞　She will (lie/lay) the book down.

Tense tells us it is present since the forms are simple.
Trial:　She will (place) the book down. (sounds OK, transitive)
Thus:　She will lay the book down.

The word *PUT* can be used interchangeably with *PLACE* as a substituter.

☞　She will (put) the book down.
☞　The paper (put) on the step.

Form POSSESSIVES of the following NOUNS.

1. Charles   2. cows   3. dress   4 Tony

Give the OTHER FOUR FORMS of the following VERBS.

5. creep   6. open   7. dig   8. forsake

9-14. For each sentence below do the following:
    a) Divide each sentence into SUBJECT and PREDICATE in the usual manner.
    b) Write all Pp's.
    c) Write S along with the simple subjects and V or LV with the Vbw's.
    d) Give the basic pattern of the sentence.
    e) Punctuate if needed.

9. The evening stars reflected on the smooth calm water of the lake.

10. It was a beautiful night at the old lakeside resort.

11. The two sweethearts wandered slowly along the lakeside path.

12. From behind a tree to one side two younger brothers spied on the lovers.

13. These mischievous lads had a great prank in mind for their sister.

Correct each sentence below with punctuation and/or proper words.

14. Bill your dog is setting on the couch again.

15. Yes I will raise the flag at 6:30 on Tuesday December 15.

Write sentences which fit the formulas below; tie them together into a single story or description. Use subjects which contain more than two words.

16. Pp S V O Pp.

17. S Pp V Pp Pp.

18. S V Pp Pp.

19. Pp S V O Pp Pp.

20. S LV Asc Pp.

```
┌─────────────────────────────────────────────────────────────┐
│                        DEFINITION                             │
│   APPOSITIVE (APPOS) - a noun or a pronoun acting as a noun that │
│       follows another noun to explain or rename it.           │
└─────────────────────────────────────────────────────────────┘
```

An appositive is the second name for the same thing. The first noun identifies the item, and the second noun simply gives it a second name. The appositive is the second noun; it can also be called the noun in apposition.

     ☞ Harry, my brother, is a great guy.
     ☞ Last night we had tacos, our favorite meal.

Sometimes the appositive can be linked to the first noun with the conjunction *OR*.

     ☞ The king's chair, or throne, was at the end of the room.

☞ **NOTE: The appositive is set off from the rest of the sentence with commas.** The appositive and all of its modifiers should be included within the commas.

     ☞ The record, a real oldie from the 1950's, sounded pretty scratchy.

The case of the appositive will mimic the case of the noun it follows. Thus, if the first noun is nominative, the appositive will be nominative also. If the first noun is objective case, the appositive will also be objective. This is of little concern when using nouns in the appositive since nouns do not show case, but **it is necessary to know when using pronouns in the appositive.**

     ☞ We picked two girls, you and her, to represent us.
     ☞ The club awarded two members, him and me, with certificates.
     ☞ One student, he, will go for the paper.

☞ **NOTE:** The **case of the first noun determines** which **form of the pronoun** must be used. The above sentences are correct as written. **Be careful to check the case when using a pronoun in the appositive.**

It should be evident that **any noun in its normal function can have an appositive excepting the nouns that function as modifiers.** In practice most of the appositives will appear after a subject or a direct object.

    ☞   S   The dog, a hound, was fast on the trail.
    ☞   O   He caught the scent, a feline odor, right away.
    ☞   SC   The cat was a big one, a real trophy.
    ☞   OP   The cat was resting in a tree, a leafy oak.
    ☞   IO   The hunter gave his wife, a pretty lass, the claws for earrings.

We will use APPOS as the abbreviation for APPOSITIVE in certain places, especially in the formula writing. Remember to always put commas around the appositive in your writing.

Form the POSSESSIVES of the following NOUNS.

   1. Nancy   2. students   3. Tim Foss   4. people

Give the OTHER FOUR FORMS of the following VERBS.

   5. freeze   6. shoot   7. pry   8. catch

9-15.   For each sentence below do the following:
    a) Divide each sentence into SUBJECT and PREDICATE in the usual manner.
    b) Write all Pp's.
    c) Write S along with the simple subjects and V or LV with the Vbw's.
    d) Give the basic pattern of the sentence.
    e) Punctuate if needed.

9. The greatest show on earth the circus was coming to town.

10. All of the local boys and girls were quite happy about it.

11. After the first announcement in the paper one boy read magic books.

12. He practiced many tricks some very clever ones for quite some time.

13. The boy became a circus magician in his later years.

Correct each sentence below with punctuation and/or proper words.

14. Well the old boy his dog and his cat went to sea.

15. On the 4th of April in 1975 four flares big ones were lighted atop the armory.

Write sentences which fit the formulas below; tie them together into a single story or description. Use subjects which contain more than two words.

16. Pp S APPOS V O.

17. S Pp V Pp APPOS.

18. S V Pp Pp Pp.

19. Pp S V O P OP & OP.

20. S LV Nsc Pp.

Lesson 37   <u>Compound Pronoun Usage</u>

The **case of a personal pronoun can give the user some problems** when it occurs in certain situations. We will look at three typical problem areas.

The **first situation** occurs when **a noun or personal pronoun or two personal pronouns function in a compound relationship.** The case of the second word, the pronoun in this case, should be the same as the case of the first noun or pronoun. **The easy way to figure out what is correct is to use the second element by itself. If it sounds good by itself, it is right in the combination.**

    ☞ Harry and (I/me) went to the store.
    trials: I went to the store.   Me went to the store.
    thus ⇨ Harry and I went to the store.

    ☞ He gave it to Dave and (I/me).
    trials: He gave it to I.   He gave it to me.
    thus ⇨ He gave it to Dave and me.

It is worthy to note that **the predicate nominative will be the most difficult** since it gives certain problems even when there is only one personal pronoun.

    ☞ It was (he/him) and John.
    trials: It was he. (He was it.)   It was him. (Him was it.)
    thus ⇨ It was he and John. (Nsc/PN)

The **second instance of doubling occurs when a personal pronoun directly precedes a noun.** Again use the technique of dropping the other element and trying the item by itself.

    ☞ (We/Us) boys went to the game.
    trials: We went to the game.   Us went to the game.
    thus ⇨ We boys went to the game.

    ☞ Between (we/us) boys it will be a secret.
    trials: Between we it...a secret.   Between us it...a secret.
    thus ⇨ Between us it will remain a secret.

The **third instance of difficulty is when the sentence ends with *AS* or *THAN* before a personal pronoun.** The idea here is to reinsert the verb that is insinuated from the beginning of the sentence. Again, what sounds right after the insertion usually is right.

    ☞ You know more than (they/them).   (*THEY/THEM* is compared to *YOU*.)
    trials: They know more.   Them know more.
    thus ⇨ You know more than they.

    ☞ The rain fell on the Smiths as much as (we/us). (*WE/US* is compared to *SMITHS*.)
    trials: The rain fell on we.   The rain fell on us.
    thus ⇨ The rain fell on the Smiths as much as us.

Compound Pronoun Usage

Form POSSESSIVES of the following NOUNS.

1. Betty   2. rangers   3. Arlo and Jack   4. grass

Give the OTHER FOUR FORMS of the following VERBS.

5. awake   6. run   7. force   8. draw

9-13 For each sentence below do the following:
   a) Divide each sentence into SUBJECT and PREDICATE in the usual manner.
   b) Write all Pp's.
   c) Write S along with the simple subjects and V or LV with the Vbw's.
   d) Give the basic pattern of the sentence.
   e) Punctuate if needed.

9. The galactic fleet from Arcturus was on its way to earth.

10. The command centers and military installations were very nervous.

11. It was the first visit of this sort for earth in over a thousand years.

12. In the last five hundred years even radio contact with aliens had ceased.

13. The general in command of the earth systems readied his defenses.

Correct each sentence below with punctuation and/or proper words.

14. Wow Bill and me got the best deal at the local deli last week.

15. He threw the paper to we boys laying on the sofa.

Write sentences which fit the formulas below; tie them together into a single story or description.

16. Pp Pp S Pp V O.

17. S V Pp Pp.

18. S V O Pp Pp.

19. Pp S V O APPOS.

20. S LV Asc Pp.

Lesson 38

Transformations 1: YES/NO and THERE Types

Up until now this grammar has only dealt with basic sentences in the active voice and in a regular syntax. At this point we will look at three other common types of sentences which occur in the English language.

The **first type** we will call **the Yes/No question**. We give it this name since it is a question which can be answered by *YES* or *NO*. Some questions require lengthy answers and begin with words such as *WHY* or *WHAT*. We will not consider them at this point.

Two basic methods exist for transforming a Yes/No question from a simple basic statement.

The **first method** is to simply **move the first verb in the sentence to the very front of the sentence**. It does not matter whether the first verb is a helper or a main verb; simply move it to the front of the sentence and then add a question mark.

    ☞ The boy is my friend.   Is the boy my friend?

    ☞ The store has sold out.   Has the store sold out?

    ☞ She has been eating prunes.   Has she been eating prunes?

The **second method** of making a Yes/No question is to **use a form of *DO***. The *DO* form can be added in front of the original sentence only when there is just a main verb in the sentence. If the original sentence has helping verbs, the *DO* form will not work. The *DO* form will take the form of the main verb, and the main verb will take the simple form. Remember to add the question mark at the end of the sentence.

    ☞ His bird sings all night.   Does his bird sing all night?

    ☞ The dog barked at the cat.   Did the dog bark at the cat?

The **second type of transformation we will deal with here is the THERE + BE type.** These transformations **always have *THERE* as the first word in the sentence**, and **following it will be some form of *BE*.**

The **original sentence must have a form of *BE* as a helping verb** in it. To transform the sentence, one simply adds the word *THERE* to the front of the sentence. Next move the *BE* form of the verb along with other helpers preceding it; place this/these directly behind *THERE* in the new sentence.

    ☞ The cock is crowing.   There is the cock crowing.

    ☞ A cow has been eating corn.   There has been a cow eating corn.

    ☞ Some kids are playing ball.   There are some kids playing ball.

The third type of transformation is the passive; it will be taken up in the next lesson.

Give the OTHER FOUR FORMS of the following VERBS.

1. forget   2. play   3. earn   4. sting

Transform these into YES/NO questions.

5. Six boys have eaten the big taco.
6. The ketchup oozed all over their faces.

Transform these into THERE types.

7. Four hounds are following the scent.
8. An exhibition may be going on tonight.

9-13.   For each sentence below do the following:
   a) Divide each sentence into SUBJECT and PREDICATE in the usual manner.
   b) Write all Pp's.
   c) Write S along with the simple subjects and V or LV with the Vbw's.
   d) Give the basic pattern of the sentence.
   e) Punctuate if needed.

9. The train from Timber Flats was on time each Friday with the payroll.

10. It was common knowledge in the area about the payroll shipments.

11. Usually on Fridays a large group of deputies accompanied the payroll.

12. On one specific Friday of last year only one deputy came with the money.

13. The rest of the men had gone on another job temporarily.

Correct each sentence below with punctuation and/or proper words.

14. Yes the man gave Dan and I a coupon for laying the money away.

15. We bears ran faster and farther than them.

Write sentences which fit the formulas below; tie them together into a single story or description.

16. Pp S Pp V O Pp.

17. S V O APPOS Pp.

18. S V Pp Pp.

19. Pp S LV Nsc Pp.

20. S Pp V O Pp.

Lesson 39   Transformations 2: Passives

The passive voice occurs in English about ten percent of the time or less. The vast majority of the sentences we read, speak, and hear are in the active voice. **The use of the passive enables us to focus on the action and its object rather than the subject.** In fact, the originator of the action can be totally left out, and the sentence will still make good sense.

The passive does three things to a regular sentence.
      1) It moves the object to the front.
      2) It changes the verb slightly by adding a new form.
      3) It either throws the original subject away or puts it into a prepositional phrase at or near the end of the sentence. Although the old object now occupies a subject position, the action is still directed at it.

      ☞   active   John shot the bear.
      ☞   passive   The bear was shot (by John).

You will notice that John does the shooting while the bear gets shot in both sentences. The syntax and the emphasis is what is different. The stress in the second sentence is on the action and its object.

HOW TO MAKE A PASSIVE

1) Move the original object to the front of the new sentence.

2) Add the proper form of *BE* (get tense from 1st verb in original; get agreement from new noun in subject position), and change the main verb to an *-EN* form. The *BE* form goes right in front of the main verb.

3) Optional: Add the old subject to the end of the sentence in a prepositional phrase beginning with *BY*.

      ☞ The man saw the bear.   The bear was seen (by the man).
      ☞ The dog was eating a bone.   A bone was being eaten (by the dog).
      ☞ The flute charms the snake.   The snake is charmed (by the flute).

☞ **NOTE:** If a sentence has a direct object and an indirect object, either one may be used in the new subject position. When the situation occurs, the common choice in today's English is to move the indirect object. See #1 below.

      ☞   The boy gave the girl a ring.
      #1   The girl was given the ring (by the boy).
      #2   A ring was given the girl (by the boy).

Give the OTHER FOUR FORMS of the following VERBS.

  1. charge   2. eat   3. fiddle   bring

Transform these as indicated:

5. (YES/NO) The early birds are catching the worms.

6. (THERE) Seven beauties are competing for the prize.

7. (PASSIVE) The early birds are catching the worms.

8. (PASSIVE) The dragon may eat our cow.

9-13. For each sentence below do the following:
    a) Divide each sentence into SUBJECT and PREDICATE in the usual manner.
    b) Write all Pp's.
    c) Write S over the simple subjects and V or LV over the Vbw's.
    d) Give the basic pattern of the sentence.
    e) Punctuate if needed.

9. The sloop slipped from behind the headland with great speed.

10. The cargo fluyt was unaware of the sloops presence at first.

11. A quick shot through the main rigging was their first clue.

12. It was clearly a very unhappy situation for the men on the cargo fluyt.

13. From stem to stern the merchant seamen quickly realized their plight.

Correct each sentence below with punctuation and/or proper words.

14. Well the boy shot Bill and I a dirty look as we edged away.

15. The older couple played bridge as well as us.

Write sentences which fit the formulas below; tie them together into a single story or description.

16. S Pp Pp V O & V O.

17. S APPOS V O.

18. S Pp V Pp Pp.

19. Pp Pp S LV Asc.

20. S Pp Pp V P OP & OP.

[See Additional Exercises, pages 173-175 for more practice on transformations.]

```
                              DEFINITIONS
c/c = coordinating conjunction, connectors of any two equal grammatical units
  I = independent clause, complete sentence, a grammatical unit consisting of
            subject and predicate that makes complete sense in itself

              PUNCTUATION RULE 1 = I, c/c I.
```

The c/c are easily remembered by the memory trick **FANBOYS** which stands for these words:
FOR, AND, NOR, BUT, OR, YET, SO.

The rule is simple: **when two complete thoughts are joined together by a c/c, a comma needs to go between the first independent clause and the c/c.**

      ☞ Sam went to the store, and he bought a loaf of bread.

☞ **NOTE 1:** Please see that *AND* and *OR* are often used to connect equal items that are not sentences. In such cases the comma does not generally occur unless a series of items is present.

☞	(words)	big and fat
		running and jumping
☞	(phrases)	over the river and through the woods
		running the track or throwing the discus
		ate the bread and drank the milk
☞	(clauses)	when he fell and as he struck

☞ **NOTE 2:** The word *FOR* can also be used as a preposition. Be careful to check that what follows is an independent clause and not a noun with a modifier or two.

☞	(prep)	He went to town for his morning breakfast.
☞	(c/c)	He wanted to eat, for he was hungry.

☞ **NOTE 3:** The word *NOR* affects the order of the words behind it, and they will have the sound of a question instead of a statement.

      ☞ He did not want a horse, nor did he want a cow.

The best way to use the rule is to look for key words, any of the FANBOYS, and then check to see that a complete sentence is on both sides. If so, insert a comma directly prior to the c/c.

      ☞ Albert wanted to eat breakfast and requested it early.   (no comma)
      ☞ Albert wanted to eat breakfast, and he requested it early.   (comma)

In the first sentence the words following the c/c do not make a complete sentence by themselves; thus, no comma is used. In the second sentence the words after the c/c make very good sense by themselves. In this case we know that there are two independent clauses being put together with a c/c, so we should put the comma between the first clause and the c/c.

Give the OTHER FOUR FORMS of the following VERBS.

  1. run   2. fight   3. train   4. fly

Transform these as indicated:

5. (YES/NO) The bad dogs are digging in the garden.

6. (THERE) The cows were coming in from the pasture.

7. (PASSIVE) The early birds have caught the worms.

8. (PASSIVE) The dragon will be eating our cow.

9-13. For each sentence below do the following:
      a) Divide each sentence into SUBJECT and PREDICATE in the usual manner.
      b) Write/bracket all Pp's.
      c) Write S along with the simple subjects and V or LV with the Vbw's.
      d) Give the basic pattern of the sentence.
      e) Punctuate if needed.

9. The trained eagle waited patiently for his handler a man from Grimsby.

10. The eagle could soar across mountains and seas with ease.

11. In the last rays of the evening sun the riding master appeared.

12. He was clearly happy about something and it showed on his face.

13. The riding master approached the eagle and spoke softly to it.

Correct each sentence below with punctuation and/or proper words.

14. A fine generous man gave Jim and I a chance to earn some money.

15. The other runner was just a bit quicker than me.

Write sentences which fit the formulas below; tie them together into a single story or description.

16. Pp S Pp V & V O.

17. S V O Pp c/c S V O.

18. S Pp V Pp Pp.

19. Pp Pp S LV Nsc.

20. S Pp Pp V O c/c Pp S V O Pp.

Lesson 41   Major Punctuation 2: I sub I.

> **DEFINITION**
>
> **sub = subordinating conjunction, a word that joins two thoughts together but makes one dependent on the other**
>
> **PUNCTUATION RULE 2 = I sub I**

For this rule you will need to know another small list of words; they are called **SUBORDINATORS**. We will refer to a subordinator as **sub**. Following is a list of subordinators; the list does not cover all possible instances but is good for normal use.

as	if	because	though	although
while	when	where	unless	
since	before	after	until	
as if	so that	whereas		

The words in the third row can also be prepositions. To check whether they are functioning as prepositions or subordinators, simply see what follows the word in question. If what follows is a noun and verb combination that makes a complete thought, the word is functioning as a subordinator. If only a noun and its modifiers follow, the construction is not a sentence; thus, the word would be functioning as a preposition.

☞ after the big game   (prep)

☞ after the game was over   (sub)

The subordinators in the fourth row are composed of two words, but they function as a unit whether they are connected or separate.

It is just as important to know where NOT to put a comma as it is to know where to use one correctly. Rule #2 is an example of knowing when not to use a comma. A subordinator causes one idea to become dependent on another. The link between the ideas becomes strong, and no punctuation is needed.

☞ He went to the doctor because he was sick.   (sub)

☞ He went to the doctor, and he was sick.   (c/c)

The word *AS* may be used to connect fragments; in such a case it would not be a subordinator. Once again the key is to see if a complete sentence follows the word in question. **Neither use here should have a comma.**

☞ He ran straight as an arrow.   (no sub)

☞ He ran to the barn as the car came into the driveway.   (sub)

Give the OTHER FOUR FORMS of the following VERBS.

1. flee   2. sing   3. wander   4. solo

Form POSSESSIVES of the following NOUNS.

5. Jane   6. Bill and Al   7. pickles   8. Jones

Transform these as indicated.

9. (PASSIVE) The early birds may catch the worms.

10. (PASSIVE) The dragon has eaten our cow.

For each of the sentences below (11-15) do the following:
   a) Divide each sentence into SUBJECT and PREDICATE in the usual manner.
   b) Write all Pp's.
   c) Write S along with the simple subjects and V or LV with the Vbw's.
   d) Give the basic pattern of the sentence.
   e) Punctuate if needed.

11. The eagle turned his head when his riding master approached.

12. The eagle ruffled his feathers and made a sound deep in his throat.

13. The man was small and agile and he mounted the eagle quickly.

14. The eagle was quite eager and spread out his wings with anticipation.

15. The rider gave a signal and the eagle hopped and flapped his wings.

Write sentences which fit the formulas below; tie them together into a single story or description.

16. Pp S Pp V sub S V O.

17. S V Pp c/c S V O.

18. Pp S V Pp Pp.

19. Pp S Pp LV Asc.

20. S Pp V c/c Pp S V Pp.

PUNCTUATION RULE 3 = Sub I, I

This rule also calls for recognizing the subordinators. This rule is different from the two previous rules in that the key word does NOT come between the two independent clauses. The comma shows the break between the two thoughts because the linking word occurs elsewhere. Note that the subordinator comes in front of both independent clauses, but those clauses are separated by a comma. The first independent clause with a subordinator on the front of it becomes a dependent clause; technically it is called an introductory subordinate clause.

Placing the subordinated clause first is handy when showing a cause and effect relationship or adding some suspense to the writing. Consider the following set of sentences.

     ☞   A) The girl screamed when she saw the shadow moving towards her.

     ☞   B) When she saw the shadow moving towards her, the girl screamed.

Physically the only differences between the two sentences are the relative placement of the subordinated clause and the punctuation. In A) it is I sub I while in B) it is Sub I, I. The meanings of the two sentences are identical, but the impacts are different. In A) the action the girl takes comes before what caused her to take it. In B) the cause precedes the action; this is a natural order and somewhat suspenseful as well. Note that both sentences are correct; a writer's choice is determined by style and preference according to each situation.

HOW TO USE THIS RULE

First, find the key word. It will be the first word in a sentence unless there are more than two independent clauses present. **Next, cover the key word and read until the obvious break; that is where the comma goes.** Be careful with those subordinators that can also function as prepositions. There must be a complete sentence (I) following the subordinator in order to use Rule #3.

     ☞ After the game we went to the hotel for dinner.   (*After* = prep)

     ☞ After the game was over, we went to the hotel for dinner.   (*After* = sub)

     ☞ **NOTE:** The first example does not have a comma whereas the second example does have a comma.

Give the OTHER FOUR FORMS of the following VERBS.

  1. stand   2. slay   3. forget   4. acquire

Form POSSESSIVES of the following NOUNS.

  5. Mary   6. Mel Burns   7. dogs   8. lady

Transform these as indicated.

  9. (PASSIVE) The fast dogs have caught the cat.

10. (PASSIVE) The dragon is eating our cows.

For each sentence below (11-15) do the following:
    a) Divide the sentence into Subject and PREDICATE in the usual manner.
    b) Write all Pp's.
    c) Write S along with the simple subjects and V or LV with the Vbw's.
    d) Give the basic pattern of the sentence.
    e) Punctuate if needed.

11. As the eagle and rider took off some guards came after the man.

12. They drew their bows and fired on the pair in the sky.

13. The man leaned low over the back of the eagle as it went higher.

14. No arrows found their marks but some came very close.

15. The pair soon flew out of range so the guards returned to town.

Write sentences which fit the formulas below; tie them together into a single story or description.

16. Sub S Pp Pp V S V O.

17. S V Pp c/c S V O.

18. Pp Pp S V Pp Pp.

19. Pp S APPOS LV Asc.

20. S Pp V sub Pp S V Pp.

```
┌─────────────────────────────────────────┐
│  ┌───────────────────────────────────┐  │
│  │                                   │  │
│  │   PUNCTUATION RULE 4  =  I; I.    │  │
│  │                                   │  │
│  └───────────────────────────────────┘  │
└─────────────────────────────────────────┘
```

This rule introduces the **use of the semicolon.** The correct use of the semicolon is a hallmark of a competent writer or at least a competent punctuator. Rules 4 and 5 both utilize the semicolon and account for most of its occurrences in normal writing. Rule 4 is very simple; **the semicolon appears between two independent clauses at the obvious break.**

> ☞ The dog ran around the house; he sniffed along the fence.
> ☞ The dog ran around the house. He sniffed along the fence.

The semicolon is a very weak link; the two independent clauses are merely punctuated as one sentence instead of two. **Note** that there is **NO KEY WORD when Rule 4 is applied.**

HOW TO USE THIS RULE

Read through the sentence until an obvious break occurs; read what is left. **If no key words** are apparent **and if the material on both sides of the break forms independent clauses, then a semicolon should be placed in the break.**

☞ **NOTE:** The lengths of the independent clauses are not restricted in any way although some similarity in length helps balance a sentence.

> ☞ The dog growled; he then barked at the intruder slinking along
> the fence under the cover of darkness.

The first independent clause is only three words; the second clause stretches to fifteen words. The sentence is out of balance, but the punctuation is correct. **Proper balance is reflective of good writing style.** Proper punctuation reveals control of the mechanical aspects of writing, but it should also help a better style to develop.

Give the OTHER FOUR FORMS of the following VERBS.

1. search   2. try   3. wear   4. leave

Form POSSESSIVES of the following NOUNS.

5. Meg & Sam   6. man   7. men   8. girls

Transform these as indicated.

9. (PASSIVE) The gopher has eaten all of the carrots.

10. (PASSIVE) One lion is killing the calves.

For each sentence below (11-15) do the following:
   a) Divide each sentence between the SUBJECT and PREDICATE in the usual manner.
   b) Write all Pp's.
   c) Write S along with the simple subjects and V or LV with the Vbw's.
   d) Give the basic pattern of the sentence; do not include Pp's.
   e) Punctuate if needed.

11. A pale sun winked through the cloudy sky at dawn.

12. A pair of weary hunters peered from under a makeshift lean-to.

13. When they saw nothing unusual they came forth from their rude cover.

14. The day did not look good but they would do their best in spite of it.

15. The two turned to the trail and moved quickly into the underbrush.

Write sentences which fit the formulas below; tie them together into a single story or description.

16. Pp Pp S V sub S V O.

17. S Pp V c/c S Pp V O Pp.

18. S Pp Pp V Pp Pp.

19. Sub S Pp LV Asc S V O.

20. S V Pp sub S Pp V O Pp.

Lesson 44   <u>Major Punctuation 5: I; c/a, I.</u>

> **DEFINITION**
> **c/a = conjunctive adverb, a weak connector requiring punctuation on both sides**
>
> **PUNCTUATION RULE 5 = I; c/a, I**

This is the fifth and final rule of major punctuation. It is also **the most complicated** since it **has two variations.** The **c/a** stands for CONJUNCTIVE ADVERB. The common conjunctive adverbs are listed below.

however	in fact	moreover	therefore
hence	consequently	nevertheless	thus
similarly	nonetheless	likewise	

These are **typical adverbs** and **are mobile** and can be found at the beginning of the second clause, somewhere in the middle of the second clause, or at the end of the second clause.

☞ I like her; **however,** she does not like me.	I; c/a, I.
☞ I like her; she, **however,** does not like me.	I; xxx, c/a, xxx.
☞ I like her; she does not, **however,** like me.	I; xxx, c/a, xxx.
☞ I like her; she does not like me, **however.**	I; I, c/a.

The first example follows the I; c/a, I rule exactly. The second and third examples place the conjunctive adverb inside the second independent clause. This is a variation on the basic rule and might be symbolized as I; xxx, c/a, xxx where the xxx stands for words found on either side. The fourth example puts the c/a at the very end of the second independent clause. This variation is symbolized as I; I, c/a.

☞ **NOTE: A semicolon always follows directly after the first independent clause no matter where the conjunctive adverb appears.**

☞ **NOTE: The conjunctive adverb is always separated from the rest of the sentence by punctuation on both sides;** the punctuation will be a semicolon and comma, two commas, or a comma and a period.

Perhaps it will become obvious that the use of a conjunctive adverb just adds another element to the I; I rule, and the added element, the c/a, needs to be set off from the rest of the sentence with extra punctuation.

In practice the use of a conjunctive adverb at the end of a sentence is falsely emphatic and usually reflects poor style. It is, however, good to know the proper punctuation anyway. It is also best not to have a conjunctive adverb as the first word in a new sentence since jumping back across a period is not its intended function.

☞ poor style:	I like her. She dislikes me, however.
	I like her. However, she dislikes me.
☞ good style:	I like her; however, she dislikes me.
	I like her. She, however, dislikes me.
	I like her; she, however, dislikes me.

Give the OTHER FOUR FORMS of the following VERBS.

  1. leap   2. reap   3. creep   4. bundle

Form POSSESSIVES of the following NOUNS.

  5. kite   6. Arne   7. Joe & Pat   8. crews

Transform these as indicated.

  9. (PASSIVE) The fast cat has eluded the barking dogs.

10. (PASSIVE) The farmers are roasting a pig.

For each sentence below (11-15) do the following:
    a) Divide between the SUBJECT and PREDICATE in the usual manner.
    b) Write all Pp's.
    c) Write S along with the simple subjects and V or LV with the Vbw's.
    d) Give the basic pattern of the sentence; don't include Pp's.
    e) Punctuate if needed.

11. The grass was thick and high nevertheless the man moved quickly.

12. No path existed in this part of the prairie but the man moved surely.

13. He was red in color and had much of his hair in a knot on one side.

14. As he moved a pattern became obvious he was searching for something.

15. He held an old rifle in one hand it was however a superior weapon.

Write sentences which fit the formulas below; tie them together into a single story or description.

16. Sub S Pp V S V Pp.

17. S V Pp c/a S V O.

18. Pp Pp S V O Pp Pp.

19. S Pp Pp LV Asc.

20. S Pp V O Pp c/c Pp S V Pp.

Lesson 45   Major Punctuation 6: Combinations

In certain instances more than two independent clauses may be combined in one sentence. If this is the case, the rules are simply applied in tandem fashion. In other words, take the first two clauses and apply the proper rule; then take the second and third clause and apply the proper rule to them as if the first clause did not exist.

☞ Note the examples below and the rules which are used.

    1. Al went to the store; he saw some tomatoes, and he bought them.
       (I; I then I, c/c I)

First we took the first two clauses, *Al went to the store* and *he saw some tomatoes*. The I; I rule applied. Then we took the second and third clauses, *he saw some tomatoes* along with *and he bought them*. In this case we found *AND* between the two complete ideas, so we applied the I, c/c I rule.

    2. Jack went to town after he fixed the car, but it still ran poorly.
       (I sub I then I, c/c I)

    3. Sam bought his lunch before he went to the bank; however, he was still out of money.
       (I sub I then I; c/a, I)

    4. Sue saw the dress in the window, and she liked it very much, so she purchased it without delay.
       (I, c/c I then I, c/c I)

    5. When Fritz ate the taco, he felt satisfied, but then he saw the hamburger and French fries.
       (Sub I, I then I, c/c I)

    6. After Dan lost the bet, he vowed never to play again because he had learned his lesson.
       (Sub I, I then I sub I)

When two different types of key words are used immediately following one another, this affects punctuation. In practice the common combination is a c/c followed by a sub. In the examples note that **the c/c + sub combination requires no punctuation**. The reasoning is that the c/c is not connecting two equal items since the clause including the subordinator is dependent instead of independent. **It is easiest to simply treat the c/c + sub combination as a sub by itself.** Note the following combinations of *BUT IF*, and *AND BECAUSE*.

    ☞ You should earn a good profit but if you don't, it will be your own fault.

    ☞ Henry liked Alice because she was very pretty and because she had a gentle spirit.

In a c/a + sub combination, both key words exert an influence. The c/a will need its normal punctuation; the sub only affects the clause following it. The example here is *HOWEVER, IF*.

    ☞ Joe may be the leader; however, if he won't follow the rules, he will be deposed.

Other combinations of key words are relatively uncommon and will not be considered in this text.

Give the OTHER FOUR FORMS of the following VERBS.

1. plead   2. wash   3. think   4. feel

Transform these as indicated.

5. (PASSIVE) That sly dog may outfox those rabbits.

6. (PASSIVE) The executive officer is running both shows.

Punctuate the following sentences.

7. It was dawn of the third day when the commandos began to show up in force at the abandoned mine in the mountains.
8. The rendezvous point was located in an area with a good field of fire in all directions except one moreover it was quite secluded.
9. The partisans had arranged a good hiding spot and they had prepared well for this occasion a well-timed sabotage act of major proportions.
10. In the narrow valley in the canyon to the south of the mine the commander placed a man with a radio to relay messages and keep watch.
11. A road ran across the end of that canyon any expected enemy movements would probably happen in that sector.
12. The force could fight if it had to but its job was to hit the strategic target and inflict as much damage as possible in that area.
13. On paper the action looked easy but if the going got tough the force could make a show for itself since they were combat hardened veterans.
14. As noon of the third day approached the force seemed to undergo a change they grew thoughtful as the hour of attack came closer.
15. It would be a great surprise to the enemy nevertheless the risk was great and everyone knew some of them would not survive the day.

Write sentences that fit the formulas below; tie them together into a single story or description.

16. Sub S V O Pp S V Pp.

17. S V Pp O c/c S V O Pp.

18. Pp Pp Pp S LV Asc.

19. S Pp Pp V Pp O Pp.

20. S Pp V O S V Pp c/a.

[See *Jensen's Punctuation* for a complete treatment of major punctuation and all other punctuation.]

Lesson 46　　　　Relative Patterns 1: Introduction

```
                              DEFINITION

       R = RELATIVE = who, whom, whose, which, that (+ whoever, whomever)
              Rp = RELATIVE PATTERN (relative clause)
```

☞ **NOTE: Rp's are not sentences by themselves; they must occur in a sentence.** A relative pattern by itself is a sentence fragment.

Items of concern:

1. **Rp's usually begin with a relative.** In certain cases the relative is dropped; consequently, those clauses do not begin with a relative since none is visible.
2. **Rp's can function as either a modifier of a noun or as a noun substitute**; noun modifier is the most common function.
3. As **noun substitutes**, they will **not** be separated from the sentence with any punctuation.

   ☞ You know that bananas are fattening.

4. As a **noun modifier**, they will be separated only if the noun they are modifying is specific.

   ☞ We traced the person who had ordered the tickets.
   ☞ We asked Jim Brown, who had ordered the tickets.

☞ NOTE: When *THAT* is the relative, 1) the Rp rarely needs commas, and 2) the relative can be dropped.

   ☞ I counted the money (that) I had left.

5. *WHOSE* is possessive; it substitutes for words like *HIS, MY, YOUR, HER,* and *THEIR.*
   WHOM is used to replace objects; think *HIM.*
   WHO is used to replace subjects and subject complements; think *HE.*
   All of the above refer to people or named beings. (Fido)
   WHICH refers to things or places, NEVER to people.

```
                 HOW TO CREATE A RELATIVE CLAUSE (PATTERN)

          source              consumer                directions

        S) I like pie.     C)  The pie is good.     Rp of S; place in C

     1. Find the related item by looking for what is mentioned in both sentences.    (pie)

     2. Replace the related item in the source sentence (S) with the proper relative.
           (I like pie becomes I like which)

     3. Move the relative to the front. (It may already be there.)  This is a completed Rp.
           (I like which becomes which I like)

     4. Place the entire Rp directly behind the related item in the consumer (C) sentence.
           (The pie [which I like] is good.)
```

Rp's 1: Introduction

Give the OTHER FOUR FORMS of the following VERBS.

1. race
2. fear
3. throw
4. sting

Transform these as indicated.

5. (PASSIVE) That fat chicken may eat those early worms today.

6. (PASSIVE) Five men were operating the Ferris wheel.

Punctuate the following sentences.

7. A swarm of bees surrounded the man on the vines but he didn't seem to pay them any mind at all.
8. As he hung from the vine with one hand he was jabbing a long stick into the cliff-side hole where the hive was.
9. Under the small shelf in a large crack the comb was quite visible the people standing eighty feet below could clearly see it.
10. The man on the vines made it look easy every one knew however that his movements and calm took years of practice to perfect.

A. The bees swarmed around the man.
B. The man was hanging on the vines.

C. The bees were guarding the honey.
D. Their hive was in a crack.

11. Rp of A; place in C.

12. Rp of B; place in A.

13. Rp of A; place in B.

14. Rp of D; place in A.

15. Rp of C; place in A.

Write sentences that fit the formulas below; tie them together into a single story or description.

16. Pp S V O Pp c/a S V Pp.

17. S V Pp c/c S V O Pp.

18. Pp Pp Pp S V O Pp.

19. S Pp Pp V Pp O Pp.

20. Sub S V O S V Pp.

WHO and *WHOM* are two relatives used for people or at times for pets or animals that have known personalities and identities. The correct use of these two relatives is rather easy to master once the relationship is understood.

The key to understanding which relative to use is knowing the use of the noun it is replacing. *WHO* is used to replace nouns in the subjective or nominative case. That means *WHO* replaces subjects and subject complements. On the other hand, *WHOM* is used to replace nouns in the objective or accusative case. That means *WHOM* is used to replace nouns being used as some kind of object, either direct, indirect, or prepositional.

Look at the five sentences listed below as examples. The focus will be on *THE MAN* as the item to be replaced.

    ☞   A. The man went to the store.
    ☞   B. We saw the man on the sidewalk.
    ☞   C. The storekeeper walked over near the man.
    ☞   D. Their best customer was the man.
    ☞   E. The cashier gave the man some change.

If the above sentences were to be used as source sentences for forming relative clauses, sentences A and D would use *WHO* to replace *THE MAN* because *THE MAN* is used in the nominative case in both sentences. The other three sentences would use *WHOM*.

A clever device to help know which relative to use is to substitute certain traditional pronouns. *HE* and *THEY* tell that *WHO* will be the correct form. *HIM* and *THEM* identify *WHOM* as the proper form. Please note that female and neuter pronouns do not correspond as well; just substitute one of the above. Also note that one set of the three forms all end with *M*; that is how to easily remember them.

Sentence A above could easily be rendered He went to the store; thus, the relative clause would be who went to the store.

Likewise, sentence B above could read We saw him on the sidewalk; hence, the relative clause would be whom we saw on the sidewalk.

Similarly it is now obvious that *HE* would best substitute in sentence D while *HIM* is the better choice for sentences C and E.

The easiest way to remember when to use *WHO* or *WHOM* is just to try *HIM* or *THEM* to see if *WHOM* is the form to use. If the sentence does not work well with the *M* forms, *WHO* will be form of the relative to use.

Give the OTHER FOUR FORMS of the following VERBS.

1. crack   2. sing   3. bring   4. do

Transform these as indicated:

5. (PASSIVE) The old horse has plowed three acres today.

6. (PASSIVE) Five girls are cleaning the kitchen.

Punctuate the following sentences.

7. A school of fish swam through the water near the nose of the boat the man at the helm however could not see them.
8. When the boy in the front of the boat looked to his right he could see shadows moving through the water.
9. With the sun reflecting on the water it was difficult to see well nevertheless the boy determined that it was a school of bass.
10. The boy signaled to his father and began maneuvering his pole into position his father cut the motor and got his own line into position.

A. The man swam around the girl.   C. The man was looking for fish.
B. The girl was floating in the water.   D. His reasons were good.

11. Rp of A; place in C.

12. Rp of B; place in A.

13. Rp of A; place in B.

14. Rp of D; place in A.

15. Rp of C; place in A.

Write sentences that fit the formulas below; tie them together into a single story or description.

16. Sub S V O Pp S V Pp.

17. S V Pp c/a S V O Pp.

18. Pp S V O c/c S V O Pp.

19. Pp S V O sub S V Pp Pp.

20. Pp Pp S V O Pp Pp.

Lesson 48   Relative Patterns 3: Punctuation

Punctuation of relative clauses falls under the general category of restrictive vs. non-restrictive modifiers. Other names for the same categories are essential vs. non-essential and necessary vs. parenthetical modifiers.

The tip-off for using commas with relative clauses is whether or not the noun which directly precedes the relative clause **is a specific or general noun.** In most cases that translates to **whether or not the noun is common or proper; does it give the name of somebody or not?**

Look at the sentences listed below as examples.

    ☞ A. The man went to the store.
    ☞ B. John went to the store.
    ☞ C. The storekeeper talked to the man.
    ☞ D. The storekeeper talked to John.
    ☞ E. The cashier gave the man some change.
    ☞ F. The cashier gave John some change.

If a relative was made from any of the above sentences and placed behind *JOHN*, the relative clause would **parenthetical because *JOHN* is very specific.** The relative clause is not needed to identify the noun which in this case is *JOHN*.

    ☞ Rp of A; place in D

    ✎ The storekeeper talked to John, who went to the store.

On the other hand, when the same relative clause is placed behind a general term such as *THE MAN*, **no commas are used since the clause is essential or necessary** to help identify which man the sentence is talking about.

    ☞ Rp of A; place in C.

    ✎ The storekeeper talked to the man who went to the store.

From the above it can be seen that any relative clause following the reference *JOHN* would be set off by commas; that would apply to relative clauses put into sentences B, D, and F.

Likewise, sentences A, C, and E would have relatives that had no commas since *THE MAN* is general and not a proper name.

☞ **NOTE: If a relative clause comes somewhere in the interior of a sentence and requires commas, the relative clause will have commas on both sides of it.**

    ☞ Rp of E; place in B.

    ✎ John, whom the cashier gave some change, went to the store.

Give the OTHER FOUR FORMS of the following VERBS.

1. weave   2. sleep   3. have   4. drug

Transform these as indicated.

5. (PASSIVE) His new car has earned two trophies at the show.

6. (PASSIVE) The cub scouts are building a fire in the pit.

Punctuate the following sentences.

7. As the two men spoke the larger one seemed to leap forward into the arms of the other who was known as Crowe.
8. Crowe held the Black Slayer a moment and then dropped him there was a cloth-yard shaft protruding from the edge of the creatures helm.
9. With the arrow through the neck coif of chain mail the Black Slayer had died instantly and Crowe suddenly knew that he was in trouble.
10. Crowe who was dazed by the sudden attack made little attempt to defend himself the others however were moving and drawing weapons.

A. The knight thrust at the dragon.   C. The fire was aimed at Sir Alfric.
B. The dragon breathed fire and smoke.   D. Sir Alfric's armor was scorched.

11. Rp of A; place in B.

12. Rp of A; place in C.

13. Rp of B; place in A.

14. Rp of C; place in A.

15. Rp of D; place in A.

Write sentences that fit the formulas below; tie them together into a single story or description.

16. Pp S V O S c/a V Pp Pp.

17. S V Pp c/c S V O Pp.

18. Pp S V O sub S V O Pp.

19. Pp S V O c/a S V Pp Pp.

20. Pp Pp Pp S V O Pp.

Lesson 49   <u>Relative Patterns 4: OP Variations</u>

Relative clauses which are derived from placing a relative in place of the object of a preposition can be made in two slightly different manners. Although both methods are correct, one sounds a bit more sophisticated and upholds another grammatical rule regarding prepositions.

Consider the two sentences below.

> A. The man jumped into the water.
> B. The water was cold.

Obviously *WATER* is the related item in the two sentences. In the first sentence *WATER* functions as the object of the preposition while in the second *WATER* is the subject. If sentence A serves as the source sentence for a relative clause to be placed into sentence B, the relative clause made according to standard procedures would be as found below.

> ☞ which the man jumped into

Placing this relative clause into the source sentence would give the result below.

> ☞ The water which the man jumped into was cold.

The sentence is perfectly good and would pass in most instances. There is, however, a slightly different relative clause that could be produced from the same source sentence using *WATER* as the relative. This variation keeps the original prepositional order to the phrase. It means simply moving the prepositional phrase with the relative in it to the front of the clause.

> ☞ into which the man jumped

Placing that new variation into the consumer sentence yields the sentence below.

> ☞ The water into which the man jumped was cold.

The second sentence is correct but has the added advantage of placing the preposition in its proper positional relationship with its object. The sentence also has a more correct or grammatical ring to it. A good writer should be able to utilize this second method on a regular basis.

☞ **NOTE:** Both methods or phraseologies are correct in English today, but **the second variation which maintains the preposition and object relationship in the correct spatial order is the one to be preferred in good writing.**

Give the OTHER FOUR FORMS of the following VERBS.

1. corrupt   2. dream   3. wear   4. get

Transform these as indicated.

5. (PASSIVE) The pretty girl has baked two pies for her boyfriend.

6. (PASSIVE) The goats are tearing a hole in the fence.

Punctuate the following sentences.

7. Seutonius threw his spear into the approaching mass and grabbed his sword from its scabbard the time to fight or die had come.
8. Seutonius the line sergeant for his phalanx encouraged his men forward but they were well disciplined and needed little help at that moment.
9. As he marched forward he could see the muscles ripple under his enemies uniforms he did not hesitate however in pressing the attack.
10. Proscus who was feeling sick to his stomach did not share the zeal for battle that Seutonius and the others seemed to have.

A. Borric threw the hatchet at the door.   C. Borric's temper flared at Marsus.
B. The door was thick and made of oak.   D. Marsus was not enjoying the situation.

11. Rp of A; place in B.

12. Rp of C; place in A.

13. Rp of C; place in D.

14. Rp of B; place in A.

15. Rp of D; place in C.

Write sentences that fit the formulas below; tie them together into a single story or description.

16. S Rp V O Pp Pp.

17. S V Pp Pp c/c S V.

18. Sub S V O Pp S V Pp.

19. Pp S V O S c/a V Pp.

20. S V O Rp S V O Pp.

Lesson 50   Relative Patterns 5: S LV N Variations

Relative clauses which are derived from the S LV N pattern or which are placed into an S LV N consumer sentence always present the maker with two options. The reason for this is obvious in that the subject and the noun subject complement refer to the same item. Thus, it can be seen that the related item from another sentence has two separate words in one sentence to which it can relate.

Consider the sentences below.

> A. The man jumped into the water.
> B. The man was my brother.

Obviously *MAN* is the related item in the two sentences. In the second sentence, however, *MAN* and *BROTHER* refer to the same item, so both would relate to *MAN* in the first sentence. Although two choices exist in such situations, one may be clearly better than the other at times. Observe the two sentences below which are made using B as the source sentence.

> ☞ Rp of B; place in A

1) The man who was my brother jumped into the water.
2) The man who the man was jumped into the water.

Obviously the second sentence makes little sense even though it is a correct construction. Now further observe the two possibilities if the source and consumer sentences are reversed.

> ☞ Rp of A; place in B

1) The man who jumped into the water was my brother.
2) The man was my brother who jumped into the water.

In this case it seems that either sentence fares equally well. Perhaps the first sentence might have more adherents, but both sentences express themselves rather well and make the point.

Some more examples may help to see that the author has some discretion when handling the S LV N situations.

> A. The detective trailed the thief.
> B. The lawman was Bruno Harkon.

> ☞ Rp of A; place in B.

1) The lawman who trailed the thief was Bruno Harkon.
2) The lawman was Bruno Harkon, who trailed the thief.

> ☞ Rp of B; place in A.

1) The detective who was Bruno Harkon trailed the thief.
2) The detective who the lawman was trailed the thief.

Obviously, some options are better than others; chose wisely.

Give the OTHER FOUR FORMS of the following VERBS.

1. run   2. dig   3. tear   4. go

Transform these as indicated.

5. (PASSIVE) The owls have captured a young rabbit for their food.

6. (PASSIVE) The rabbit was eating some peas growing on the fence.

Punctuate the following sentences.

7. Flavius popped the hot dog into his mouth and then he looked down the Rue de Appia a broad avenue filled with people.
8. The city of Maxus which was thriving after the recent war was peopled by all sorts of folks these days it was an exciting time to live.
9. When Flavius finished chewing and swallowing his treat he began walking in a leisurely manner toward the harbor along the avenue.
10. A few of the taller ships masts could be seen from where he was but Flavius needed to get back on board his ship and conduct business.

A. Flavius opened the hold for his three clients.   D. Chronan's eye missed nothing in the hold.
B. The hold was full of exotic merchandise.   E. Chronan always profited from trading with Flavius.
C. Old Chronan was a shrewd trader.

11. Coordinate A with B.

12. Subordinate C; place behind D.

13. Subordinate C; place before E.

14. APPOS of C; place in E.

15. Rp of D; place in C.

16. Rp of E; place in A.

17. Rp of A; place in B.

18. Rp of B; place in D.

19. Rp of E; place in C.

20. Rp of E; place in C. (another variation)

Relative clauses are not picky about the types of sentences from which they are derived. As long as two sentences have a related item in common, a relative clause can be made from one and placed in the other. Passive sentences are no exception. Observe the sentences below.

> A. The warrior drew the sword.
> B. The sword had a very sharp blade.
> C. The warrior had a hide shield on his arm.

Obviously *sword* is the related item in the first two sentences. If the two sentences were to be placed together without transforming either of them, the results would be as expected. See the examples below for illustration.

> ☞ Rp of B; place in A.

1) The warrior drew the sword which had a very sharp blade.

> ☞ Rp of A; place in B.

2) The sword which the warrior drew had a very sharp blade.

Nothing new appeared in those examples. Now observe what happens when an extra command is given.

> ☞ Passive of A; Rp of A; place in B.

first)   The sword was drawn by the warrior.   = passive of A

then)   The sword which was drawn by the warrior had a very sharp blade.

or)   The sword which was drawn had a very sharp blade.

Either of the two variations is correct. One may be better than the other if the original subject now found in the prepositional phrase helps the meaning greatly. Of course, if the related item is in the prepositional phrase in the passive, it will have to be included. In this case we will use *warrior* as the related item.

> ☞ Passive of A; Rp of A; place in C.

The warrior by whom the sword was drawn had a hide shield on his arm.

It is true that things could get a bit complicated, but everything works out if the rules are all followed in good order.

Give the other four forms of the following verbs.

  1. fetch   2. spend   3. cast   4. weep

Punctuate the following sentences.

5. Arkady handled the bauble with ease he was so good that the people couldn't see him slip it into his sleeve.

6. It was a show for the farm folk and they never seemed to tire of it or be amazed at the basic tricks he played on them.

7. The idea was to get them to part with some of their money Arkady was not always happy with just that however.

8. His favorite trick a clever sleight of hand was to get someone to bet on which shell the pea would be under.

9. After he let them win a few he encouraged a higher bet this was to win a bunch and not fool around with them too long.

10. With the care and craft of a master Arkady would ply his trade and he usually made enough to eat and sleep under cover.

A. Arkady set the shells on the table.
B. The big farmer kept his eye on the shells.
C. Framton had seen such shows before.

D. Arkady's hand moved the shells very rapidly.
E. Arkady was a master at his trade.

11. Coordinate A with B.
12. Subordinate E; place before D.
13. Subordinate B; place behind A.
14. Appos of E; place in A.
15. Rp of D; place in A.
16. Rp of A; place in E.
17. Rp of B; place in C.
18. Passive of A; Rp of A; place in B.
19. Passive of C; Rp of C; place in B.
20. Rp of E; place in A.

Lesson 52   Relative Patterns 7: Combinations

Relative clauses are not limited to one occurrence per sentence. They can occur in a variety of combinations. There is a practical limit to sentence length which should be observed, and undue complexity in a sentence due to forced constructions is not desirable. However, good sentences can and do occur with multiple relative clauses in them. Consider the illustrations below.

> A. The warrior drew the sword.
> B. The sword had a very sharp blade.
> C. The warrior had a hide shield on his arm.
> D. The sword gleamed in the sunlight.

☞ Rp of B; Rp of C; place in A

The warrior who had a hide shield on his arm drew the sword which had a very sharp blade.

In the example it can be seen that both relative clauses had a different related item in the consumer sentence. Thus, each relative clause had its own position to occupy. The syntax of the above example is S Rp V O Rp. Note the difference in the next application.

☞ Rp of A; Rp of B; place in C.

The warrior who drew the sword which had a very sharp blade had a hide shield on his arm.

The difference in this application is that **one relative clause had to fit into another one** in order to be included in the consumer sentence. Sentence B could only relate to sentence A, but sentence A could relate to sentence C. The syntax of the resulting sentence would be as follows:

S (Rp (Rp)) V O Pp

The parentheses illustrate that the second Rp was included as part of the first Rp and that the second Rp was hooked to the first Rp. Another illustration shows yet another situation.

☞ Rp of B; Rp of D; place in A.

The warrior drew the sword which had a very sharp blade and which gleamed in the sunlight.

Note the syntax here is S V O Rp and Rp. Both of the relative clauses want to relate to the same item in sentence A. The result is that they must be placed in tandem and connected with *and* so that their equality is preserved. It is possible to leave off the second *which* since it would be understood, but keeping it is just as good in this case.

The various combinations above each serve a purpose. Being careful and following step by step procedures is the safe way to handle multiple relative clause combinations.

Punctuate the following sentences.

1. Folmer took the blow with little evidence of pain although it jarred him to his toes as he broke its force with his arm.

2. He was in for a tough scrap and he knew it even if the rest of his band had been fooled.

3. This was no ordinary merchant they had picked to victimize no this fellow who was dressed so casually was anything but a common trader.

4. Soldan smiled to himself and thought about the reward money which he should be able to collect from turning in these puny brigands.

5. If he could get this big brute down quickly the other two would just be icing on the cake and the bounty money would be his.

A. Folmer charged Soldan.   D. Soldan was an accomplished fighter.
B. The brigand had no idea of proper technique.   E. The situation did not look good for Folmer.
C. Folmer's size and power had won the battles before.

6. Coordinate C with D.
7. Subordinate B; place before A.
8. Subordinate D; place behind E.
9. Appos of D; place in A.
10. Rp of A; place in D.
11. Rp of A; place in E.
12. Rp of C; place in A.
13. Passive of A; Rp of A; place in D.
14. Passive of A; Rp of A; place in E.
15. Rp of A; Rp of D; place in E.

Write sentences that fit the formulas below; tie them together into a single story or description.

16. Pp S V O S c/a V O Rp.

17. S V Pp c/c S V O Pp.

18. Pp S V sub S V O Pp.

19. Sub S Rp V O S V Pp.

20. Pp Pp Pp S V O Rp.

[See Additional Exercises, pages 175-181 for more practice on relative clauses.]

At this time it is important to review the functions of a noun since nouns occur with regularity in some of the verbals that will be covered in the following lessons. By now it is assumed that nouns can be generally recognized and picked out when mixed with other words in sentences. **Since English is a syntactical language, one in which words relate to one another based on their relative positions, the method employed to figure out the function of a given noun will be based on position.**

The six basic functions of a noun are listed below:

S	=	subject of a sentence or clause
O	=	direct object of an active verb
OP	=	object of a preposition
SC	=	subject complement, follows a linking verb, refers to subject
IO	=	indirect object, receives the object
MOD	=	modifies another noun

Using the word *brick*, the following examples will show each use in turn.

S	The brick is red.
O	The man saw the brick.
OP	The man tripped over the brick.
SC	The lump of clay became a brick.
IO	The man gave the brick a kick.
MOD	The man built a brick wall.

It should be remembered that while a noun could possibly function in six different manners in a sentence, **any given noun in any given sentence can only do one job at one time.** In no circumstances will a noun function in two different capacities at one time.

An easy method for figuring out what specific function a noun is carrying out in a sentence is to **simply look to the left of the noun in question.** There are two types of key words to look for, prepositions and verbs. Generally the key words will be rather close, perhaps the immediate leftward word or within two or three words to the left. The method employs a process of elimination based on frequency of usage.

The basic steps in outline form are as follows:

    1) locate the noun in question
    2) look to the left
        a) if preposition is found, OP = function
        b) if active verb is found, O = function
        c) if linking verb is found, SC = function
        d) if none of the above is found, S = probable function
  ☞ NOTE #1: Under normal conditions at least one subject is necessary in each sentence.
        e) CAUTION: two other functions exist
            1. MOD: points to a noun directly to its right
            2. IO: a *give* type verb on the left and a noun on the right
  ☞ NOTE #2: Appositives assume the function of the noun they follow.

Noun Functions 5: Review

For each of the following, identify the nouns and the pronouns acting as nouns and their specific functions.

1. The old man went over to his bed and tossed his hat on the chair.
2. His hat was a Stetson, and it had an eagle feather in the band.
3. The band of the hat was made of rattlesnake skin.
4. The old man placed a good deal of value on his hat.
5. It had been a gift from his late wife and reminded him of her.

Punctuate the following sentences.

6. Praxis saw the horse round the bend at a gallop so he knew something was awry however he hoped he had nothing to fear from the rider.
7. The horse came toward him at full tilt Praxis thought it best to move off the road and avoid any confrontation.
8. As the rider became aware of Praxis he began to slow his steed a bit nevertheless it did not look as if he would stop near Praxis.
9. Praxis tried to get a good look at the rider but he was rather small and the horse was quite large in fact the rider was almost hidden.
10. In the semidarkness of the wooded road the light was none too good for viewing much at all so Praxis simply waited as the rider neared.

A. Varney rode on a big horse.
B. Steelthunder was a great war horse.

C. Varney was making an escape from Sir Cadrick.
D. Sir Cadrick had a bad reputation.

11. Rp of A; place in C.
12. Rp of C; place in D.
13. Passive of A; Rp of A; place in C.
14. Rp of A; Rp of C; place in B.
15. Rp of A; Rp of D; place in C.

Write sentences that fit the formulas below; tie them together into a single story or description.

16. S Rp V O c/c S V O Pp.

17. S V Pp sub S V Pp Pp.

18. Pp S V S V O Pp c/a.

19. Sub S V O S Rp V Pp.

20. Pp Pp Pp S V O Rp.

> **DEFINITION**
>
> **INFINITIVE = a *TO* + verb combination which either**
>   1) **substitutes for a noun or**
>   2) **modifies some part of the sentence**

The infinitive is one of three types of verbals. Verbals are a special class of words that have characteristics of two word classes at once. In fact, *verbal* means verb-like or having qualities like a verb. Although the verbal retains some of the verb qualities, it does the job of either a noun or adjective. That simply means that the verbal acts as a noun substitute or it modifies something.

The infinitive is very easy to recognize since it is always composed of two words; the first word is always *TO*, and the second word is ALWAYS A VERB IN THE SIMPLE FORM.

     ☞ to run, to eat, to play, to drive, to go, to be, to appear, to seem

At times there can be confusion since *to* also functions as a preposition. **The key is to see what follows the word *to*.** If a simple form verb follows, then the two words form an infinitive; if any other type of word follows, *to* is acting as a preposition.

     ☞ He wanted to go to the store.

In the example it is obvious that a verb follows the first *to*; thus, *to go* is an infinitive. After the second *to* there is no verb; in this case the *to* is acting as a preposition.

When **an infinitive** occurs, it **may have other words associated with it. These words plus the infinitive are called the infinitive phrase.** These associated words relate to the infinitive in a verb-like manner. This is why infinitives are called verbals.

As a general rule, almost all the words relating to the infinitive will follow the infinitive. These words will act as objects, subject complements, or adverbial modifiers to the infinitive. The adverbial modifiers are usually in the form of prepositional phrases.

The easy way to decide what goes with the infinitive is to ask the questions **who, what, when, where,** and **how** after the infinitive. Any words that answer those questions and are directly attached will be part of the phrase.

     ☞ To eat a pie with ice cream after dinner is a great delight.

To eat is the infinitive. ☞ Note that *a pie* tells **what**, *with ice cream* tells **how**, and *after dinner* tells **when**. Thus, the entire infinitive phrase in this sentence is *To eat a pie with ice cream after dinner*.

Briefly then, the infinitive is always composed of two words, ***to* plus a verb**. Sometimes words following directly after the infinitive will be part of the infinitive phrase. Such words are part of the phrase when they tell **who** or **what** the infinitive acts upon and **where, when,** or **how** the infinitive functions.

How to find the infinitive and its phrase if any:
    1) look for ***to* + verb** (beware of *to* + nonverb)
    2) decide the phrase (ask **who, what, where, when, how**)

For each of the following, identify the nouns and the pronouns acting as nouns and their specific functions.

1. The little girl was in her room with her doll and her teapot.
2. The teapot was her favorite piece of table decoration.
3. The doll was one that she liked very much.
4. The doll sat in a chair next to the girl as she poured their tea.
5. Such little parties often formed a part of her afternoons.

Identify the infinitives and bracket the infinitive phrases.

6. The doctor believed that it was too late for him to get to the hospital in time.
7. Instead he began to give orders over the phone to the attendant and told him first to put the patient into bed.
8. The next instructions were to heat some water and to sponge off his wounds.
9. The attendant put down the phone and went to work; he did all that the doctor told him to do, and then he went back to the phone.
10. It was getting to be a real ordeal, but the doctor wanted to know all the particulars; then the doctor finally said to watch him closely.

A. Albert owned a nice car.   C. Albert was expecting a challenge from Barney.
B. The Chevy was a real classic.   D. Barney had a Shelby Cobra.

11. Rp of A; place in C.
12. Rp of C; place in D.
13. Passive of A; Rp of A; place in C.
14. Rp of A; Rp of C; place in B.
15. Rp of A; Rp of D; place in C.

Write sentences that fit the formulas below; tie them together into a single story or description.

16. S V O Pp sub S V O Rp.

17. S V O Rp c/c S V Pp Pp.

18. Sub S V S Rp V O.

19. S V O S c/a V Pp.

20. Pp Pp S Rp V O Pp.

Lesson 55   Infinitives 2: Function - Modifier

The infinitive or infinitive phrase in any sentence will perform one of two general functions: modifier or noun substitute. In the **first capacity** the infinitive or infinitive phrase **is acting similarly to an adjective**. In the **second case** the infinitive or infinitive phrase **is functioning as a noun**.

When the infinitive or infinitive phrase is acting as a modifier, it may refer to or modify a noun or perhaps the whole sentence.

     ☞ The black horse was the one to place all bets on.
     ☞ To make things clear, the teacher repeated the question.
     ☞ The boys were ready to go fishing at dawn.

In each of the sentences above, the infinitive phrase is modifying something. In the first sentence, it should be obvious that the horse is being modified or talked about. In the second and third sentences, the infinitive phrases are talking about the whole idea expressed in the sentence. In the second sentence the phrase gives a reason why the teacher repeated the question. In the third sentence the readiness of the boys is being described.

There is **an easy way to tell if the infinitive or infinitive phrase is doing the job of a modifier; just drop it from the sentence. If the sentence makes sense without it, it is probably functioning as a modifier.** If the modifiers were dropped from the above example sentences, good sentences would still be left.

     ☞ The black horse is the one.
     ☞ The teacher repeated the question.
     ☞ The boys were ready.

When determining the function of an infinitive or infinitive phrase, the first thing to do is to try and drop it from the sentence. It is important that the entire infinitive phrase be included in what is dropped. If words are left in the sentence from the infinitive phrase, often the remaining sentence will not make good sense.

     ☞ They set the trap to catch the mouse.

If the entire infinitive phrase, *to catch the mouse*, is dropped, the remaining sentence is good: *They set the trap*. However, if only the infinitive is dropped, the remaining sentence does not sound right: *They set the trap the mouse*. Be sure to drop the whole infinitive phrase.

☞ Note also that **when an infinitive modifier begins a sentence, it will be set off from the rest of the sentence with a comma.** This is called an **introductory verbal**.

     ☞ To get a good berth, the lad turned in early.

This rule is true only if the introductory infinitive or infinitive phrase is acting as a modifier. Noun substitutes are not set off with commas.

For each of the following, identify the nouns and the pronouns acting as nouns and their specific functions.

1. A shaggy dog rolled around on the floor with his rubber bone.
2. The bone was quite chewed, and it had lots of miles on it.
3. The bone could normally be found in the corner or by the milk dish.
4. Arfy usually played with it whenever he came in the house.
5. He had a great time with it as he rolled and groaned and chewed.

Identify the infinitives and bracket their phrases. Identify those infinitives and/or infinitive phrases that are modifiers with the letters *Mod.*

6. It was a foolish thing to do, but we all decided it was high time to go grunion hunting at the beach.
7. We gathered our gear and jumped in our cars; we were quite impatient to get there.
8. The moon was just right; the evening was warm, and the beach to which we went was somewhat deserted.
9. We wanted to build a fire, and we needed a central area to work from.
10. We had to wait a short time, so we brought out the guitar to accompany ourselves with a few songs.

A. Farley had a pet snake.   C. Morton did not like the snake.
B. The snake was a diamondback rattler.   D. Morton thought Farley was daft.

11. Rp of A; place in D.
12. Appos of B; place in C.
13. Passive of C; Rp of C; place in A.
14. Rp of B; Rp of C; place in A.
15. Rp of A; Rp of D; place in C.

Write sentences that fit the formulas below; Tie them together into a single story or description.

16. Pp Pp S V O sub S Rp V Pp.

17. S V O Pp c/c S V O Rp.

18. S Appos V S Pp V O.

19. S V O c/a S V Pp.

20. Sub S V O Rp S V Pp Pp.

The infinitive or infinitive phrase in any sentence will perform one of two general functions: modifier or noun substitute. In the **first capacity** the infinitive or infinitive phrase **is acting similarly to an adjective.** In the **second case** the infinitive construction **is functioning as a noun.**

When the infinitive or infinitive phrase is acting as a noun substitute, it will be only do certain of the noun functions. It can be a **subject (S), direct object (O),** or **subject complement (SC).**

> ☞ To do his duty was his aim in life.
> ☞ He wanted to do his duty.
> ☞ His aim in life was to do his duty.

In each of the sentences above, the infinitive phrase *to do his duty* is substituting for a noun. In the first sentence it is acting as the subject of the sentence. In the second sentence it is acting as the object of the verb. In the third example it is functioning as the subject complement.

The method for figuring out the function of the infinitive or infinitive phrase **is to look to the left.** Looking to the left assumes the infinitive or infinitive phrase is functioning as a simple noun. The same rules apply here as they did for simple nouns. Look to the left one or two words; look for a verb, either active or linking. If the verb is active, the infinitive construction will be an object. If the verb is linking, the infinitive construction will be a subject complement. If neither of these two verb types appear on the left, the infinitive construction will be a subject of the sentence.

Remember, it is very necessary to first check to see if the infinitive construction can be dropped from the sentence. If it cannot be dropped, then the infinitive construction will be functioning as a noun substitute.

It is very important to keep the order of search correct: <u>first check for modifier</u>, then check for noun substitute by looking to the left.

Examples of infinitives functioning as objects of prepositions or indirect objects are rare if any. Don't worry about them as you will probably not see them or write them in normal situations.

It is of some note that infinitive constructions may be included inside other constructions such as relative clauses or other infinitive phrases. Examples of each are noted below.

> ☞ The dog which wanted to bite me was on the other side of the fence.
> ☞ We were eager to get the gizmo to work correctly.

In the first example the infinitive is within the relative clause, *which wanted to bite me*. In the second example it is clear that the second infinitive phrase modifies *gizmo* and is thereby a part of the first infinitive phrase.

For each of the following, identify the nouns and the pronouns acting as nouns and their specific functions.

1. The frantic flea hopped about the grass hoping for a victim.
2. A cat passed by the flea but was too far away to catch a ride.
3. A bird flew down later, but it stayed near the edge of the grass.
4. Soon Arfy showed up and plunked down on the grass within hopping distance.
5. The flea realized his chance and quickly jumped onto Arfy's back.

Identify the infinitives and bracket their phrases. Give their functions: Mod, S, O, SC.

6. Life has a lot to offer if people will just be aware of it.
7. Scripture says that to give is best, but many prefer to receive.
8. Some people believe that the only way to gain something is to take it from someone else
9. Such thinking is disadvantageous to everyone in the community of man.
10. Man ought to abide by the rules set before him, for they help him to get along with others.

A. Bostwik owned a gold mine.	C. Bostwik's wife was excited.
B. The mine was a real mother lode.	D. Bostwik loved his wife very much.

11. Rp of A; place in D.
12. Appos of B; place in A.
13. Passive of A; Rp of A; place in B.
14. Rp of B; Rp of C; place in A.
15. Sub A; place before C.

Write sentences that fit the formulas below; tie them together into a single story or description.

16. S V O Appos S Rp V Pp.

17. S V Pp c/c S V O Rp.

18. Sub S V O S V O Inf-Mod.

19. S V O c/a S V Pp.

20. S V O Pp sub S V Pp.

Lesson 57   <u>Infinitives 4: Compounds & Inserts</u>

Two other final items of concern regarding infinitive constructions should be dealt with in order to be complete.

The **first** is when **two infinitive constructions are used together in such a way that they are both of equal value.** For instance, both could be used as parts of a compound subject or object. When such a situation occurs, it is permissible to drop the second *to*, the one forming part of the second infinitive.

      ☞ To jump and run were his favorite activities.

Note that the *to* is not present in front of *run* in the above sentence, yet both *to jump* and *to run* would be considered infinitives in that sentence. In this case the two infinitives are parts of the compound subject. It would be equally permissible in the example to insert the second *to* into the sentence and read it that way as well.

      ☞ He liked to throw the ball and catch it.

In the above example the second infinitive does not exhibit the *to*, but it is understood. It should be noted that in the compound situation, the word *and* will almost always be present to indicate the equal relationship between the two infinitives; if *and* does not occur, *or* most certainly will.

      ☞ He liked to play first base or manage the bull pen.

The **second** item of concern here will be when **one infinitive construction is found within another infinitive construction.** One such situation arises when one infinitive construction acts as a modifier to part of another infinitive construction.

      ☞ To get a good seat to see the play, the man pushed his way up front.

The entire infinitive construction acting as a modifier is set off from the rest of the sentence by a comma. Within that modifier, however, is another infinitive construction consisting of *to see the play*. Proper identification of the two constructions would require double brackets.

      ☞ [To get a good seat [to see the play]], ...

In the next example the containing infinitive construction functions as a noun subject while the contained infinitive construction acts as a modifier.

      ☞ To throw the ball to get the out required great skill and accuracy.

Infinitive constructions are not really all that complicated, and they **are always quite visible due to their *to* plus VERB construction.** Watch for them and use them wisely to enhance your writing.

For each of the following, identify the nouns and the pronouns acting as nouns and their specific functions.

1. The little duckling bobbed in and out of the water near the shore.
2. The mother duck was content to watch things from land.
3. A mean bass lived in the pond and enjoyed duckling lunches at times.
4. The bass was biding his time and looking for a chance.
5. The mother duck kept the duckling near her in the shallows.

Identify the infinitives and bracket their phrases. Give their functions: Mod, S, O, SC.

6. The bass was beginning to tire of waiting for a chance to strike.
7. The bass wanted to get his lunch soon, so he idled forward.
8. The duckling was trying to catch a water bug skating on the surface, so it was not watching anything else at all.
9. The warm sun and quiet day lulled the mother duck to sleep.
10. The duckling suddenly spotted a cricket coming to get a drink, so it paddled close to shore to get a closer look.

A. Croyden drew the bow tight.   C. Croyden's aim was very steady.
B. The bow was made of yew wood.   D. The deer did not see Croyden.

11. Sub D; place before C.
12. Rp of A; place in D.
13. Passive of A; Rp of A; place in B.
14. Rp of C; place in A.
15. Rp of D; Rp of B; place in A.

Write sentences that fit the formulas below; tie them together into a single story or description.

16. S V O Inf-Mod.

17. Pp Pp S V O S c/a V O Pp.

18. S V O sub S V O Rp.

19. S V O c/c S Rp V O.

20. Sub S Appos V O S V Pp.

The infinitive constructions almost always begin with an infinitive.

The infinitive is composed of two parts, the word *to* and a simple verb.

      ☞ to go, to run, to eat, to play, to sleep, to exist

Remember that *to* is sometimes a preposition; check to see if a verb directly follows the *to* as that is necessary for an infinitive.

The infinitive phrase is composed of all those words that follow after the infinitive and associate with it; these words and their modifiers will generally answer the questions **who, what, where, when,** or **how.**

      ☞ to eat the pie with ice cream, to fall over backwards in the mud

The infinitive construction will function either as a modifier or noun substitute.

When the infinitive construction functions as a **modifier**, it can be dropped from the sentence, and the sentence will still make sense.

      ☞ The man was happy *to get the job*.   ☞ The man was happy.

If the infinitive construction acting as a modifier should begin the entire sentence, it will be set off from the rest of the sentence by a comma.

      ☞ To get the job, the man waited in line for three hours.

When the infinitive construction functions as a **noun substitute**, it will generally perform one of three functions: subject (S), object (O), or subject complement (SC).

      ☞ To do his duty was his aim in life.
      ☞ He wanted to do his duty.
      ☞ His aim in life was to do his duty.

The quick method to find out which noun function the infinitive construction is emulating is to look to the left. An active verb signals an object; a linking verb signals a subject complement, and no verb signals a subject.

Follow the procedure below when looking for infinitive constructions.

    1. look for *to* + verb (beware: *to* + nonverb = preposition)
    2. decide phrase if any (who, what, where, when, how)
    3. decide function
        a) attempt to throw it out
            1) yes = MOD (modifier)
            2) no = noun substitute
        b) look to the left
            1) active verb = O (object)
            2) linking verb = SC (subject complement)
            3) no verb = S (subject)

Infinitives 5: Summation

For each of the following, identify the nouns and the pronouns acting as nouns and their specific functions.

1. An able deckhand scampered to the top of the mast very quickly.
2. The first mate sent all hands aloft on captain's orders.
3. A squall was brewing off the lee quarter, and it warranted attention.
4. The wind was whipping the sails, so they would have to be furled soon.
5. The captain was no fool, and he took no chances in these waters.

Identify the infinitives and bracket their phrases. Give their functions: Mod, S, O, SC.

6. The sun was just beginning to break over the ridge at 4:30 AM.
7. Since we wanted to get an early start, we were already up by then.
8. One of the crew was trying to get the campfire going; another attempted to make some coffee for the rest of us on the Primus.
9. We all thought about the fish we hoped to catch and were eager to get going as soon as possible.
10. We guessed it to be about 25 degrees outside, but we weren't going to let a little cold weather stop our fishing.

A. Grogan was a bad outlaw.
B. Grogan's name struck fear into the travelers.

C. The Mountie was chasing Grogan.
D. Grogan hated almost everyone.

11. Rp of D; place in A.
12. Appos of A; place in D.
13. Passive of C; Rp of C; place in A.
14. Rp of B; Rp of C; place in D.
15. Sub A; place before D.

Write sentences that fit the formulas below; tie them together into a single story or description.

16. Inf-Mod S V O Rp.

17. Sub S V O S V O Pp.

18. S V O S V O c/a.

19. S V O sub S Rp V O.

20. Pp Pp S V O c/c S V Pp.

Lesson 59 Gerunds 1: Form & Function

> ## DEFINITION
>
> **GERUND = an *-ING* form of a verb which substitutes for a noun**

The **gerund** is a second verbal; like the infinitive, it is **a word that retains some of its verb characteristics while it does the job of a noun.** An accurate description or definition of a gerund is an *-ING* form of a verb which substitutes for a noun.

Gerunds in fact are really quite simple. They **only have one form** in which they ever appear, **the *-ING* form**, and they **always take the place of a noun**.

The *-ING* forms of verbs occur in normal English on a regular basis. The difficulty for English students is that only some of the words ending in *-ING* are gerunds. The method for eliminating non-gerunds is, however, not too troublesome. **The first step** is to simply toss aside those words that happen to end in *-ING* but are not actually the *-ING* forms of a verb.

> ☞ *thing*, *spring*, *morning* and certain base verb forms such as *ring*

Test this by simply cutting off the *-ING* from the rest of the word and see if a decent base verb is left. These spelling likenesses are rarely any trouble.

The second step is to see if the *-ING* form is functioning as a true verb in the sentence. To do this, it is necessary to look to the left and see if a form of *BE* is present. See the example below.

> ☞ Eating two pies at once was an ordeal.
> ☞ He was eating both pies at once.
> ☞ The boys obviously enjoyed eating both pies.

In all three sentences, *eating* is the only *-ING* word. In the first sentence no word in the sentence can precede it since it is the first word in the sentence. In the second sentence *was*, a form of *BE*, precedes *eating*, so here the word *eating* is a true verb. In the final example no form of *BE* precedes the suspect *eating*, so it is not a true verb and is therefore a verbal, perhaps a gerund.

One more step is necessary to decide if the *-ING form* is a gerund; attempt to throw it out of the sentence. **Noun substitutes can not be dropped from the sentence without a sizable loss in meaning.** Of course the gerund and its phrase must be dealt with as an entirety.

Gerunds and infinitives have the same properties when it comes to the words associated with them; the same questions are asked: **who, what, where, when,** and **how.** Whatever follows the verbal and answers any of those questions is part of the verbal phrase. If the verbal phrase is a gerund phrase, the word *it* can usually be satisfactorily substituted into the sentence.

> ☞ It was an ordeal.   The boys obviously enjoyed it.

Gerunds can substitute for nouns in any of the four following positions: (S) subject, (O) direct object, (SC) subject complement, and (OP) object of a preposition. Looking to the left of the gerund will tell what function the gerund is taking on in the sentence.

Gerunds 1: Form & Function

For each of the following, identify the nouns and the pronouns acting as nouns and their specific functions.

1. The arrow whisked through the air with little noise.
2. The archer watched it fly toward the target limb on the message tree.
3. When the arrow would hit, the archer below the tree would hear it.
4. Then he would turn and send another arrow on to another site.
5. In this way the message of alarm would be transmitted quickly.

Identify the gerunds and bracket their phrases. Give their functions: S, O, SC, OP.

6. Hearing the thunk above him caused the man clad in green to look up.
7. An arrow quivered in the limb, a signal that the king and his men were coming to this section of forest.
8. The archer drew his bow and fired it toward a gathering in the hollow.
9. The arrow was heading right for the chimney, and the men there were resting and lying about on the grass.
10. The clanking of the arrow on the chimney signaled the men in the hollow to ready themselves for action.

A. Gelwynn could shoot the bow well.
B. Gelwynn's arrows flew straight and true.

C. The sheriff wanted Gelwynn.
D. Gelwynn melted into the woods.

11. Sub C; place before D.
12. Rp of B; place in A.
13. Rp of C; place in A.
14. Rp of A; Rp of B; place in C.
15. Passive of C; Rp of C; place in D.

Write sentences that fit the formulas below; tie them together into a single story or description.

16. Sub S Rp V O S V O.

17. Pp Pp S V O Pp Pp.

18. Ger-S V O S c/a V O Pp.

19. S Rp V O sub S V O.

20. Inf-Mod S V O c/c S V Pp.

Lesson 60 Gerunds 2: Subject Complements

The gerund or gerund phrase can function as a noun in any of four capacities: subject, direct object, object preposition, and subject complement. **There is a slight problem under certain circumstances when the gerund construction acts as a subject complement.**

The problem occurs when the main verb of the sentence is a form of *BE*. The catch is that *-ING* forms are normally preceded by a *BE* form, so recognizing whether or not the *-ING* form is a true verb or a gerund takes a bit of close looking.

> ☞ His favorite dog was trying to catch a fish.
> ☞ His favorite trick was trying to catch a fish.

In the two examples above, only one word is different, the subject of each sentence. In the first sentence it can be seen that the dog is actually trying to do something. In this case *trying* is the main verb in the sentence. In the second sentence, however, the subject is not doing something but it is equal to something. Note that the trick cannot do anything, but it can equal something. In this case the trick equals the act of trying to catch a fish. Thus, the second sentence has a gerund functioning as a subject complement, and the main verb is the *BE* form *was*. So, the first test is to see if a subject complement exists. Reversing the sentence order will tell us if a true SC exists.

> ☞ Trying to catch a fish was his favorite dog.　　no equality, change of meaning
> ☞ Trying to catch a fish was his favorite trick.　　equality = SC, no change of meaning

A second test to determine if the *BE* form and the *-ING* form are a helping verb and verb combination or a true verb plus a subject complement is also available. This method seeks to combine the *BE* form with the *-ING* form. By altering the two forms into one verb, it can be readily seen if a subject complement situation exists or not. Note the examples below.

> ☞ His favorite dog tried to catch a fish.
> ☞ His favorite trick tried to catch a fish.

The first example allows the combining of the two verbs quite handily; thus, the *BE* in this case is a helping verb. The second example does not make sense, so the *BE* form is the main verb since it does not combine well. Note that the combined verb applies the tense and agreement of the *BE* form to the *-ING* verb which causes the *-ING* form to be dropped.

The situation is now clear that a *BE* plus *-ING* form requires a bit of care and thought since two differing possibilities exist. The *-ING* form may be a true verb, or it may be a gerund. **The easiest way to determine which case is present is to combine the *BE* form with the *-ING* form and see if it makes sense.** Based upon that information, the other checks can be run.

Remember, look to the left of gerunds to determine their function just as was done for infinitives. **Prepositions yield object prepositions; active verbs mean direct objects; linking verbs mean subject complements, and none of the above means a subject.**

Gerunds 2: Subject Complements

For each of the following, identify the nouns and the pronouns acting as nouns and their specific functions.

1. The horse shied from the man standing in the grass by the road.
2. The knight watched the man carefully since it was dangerous territory.
3. Nobody in this area was trusted since the enemy agents had moved in.
4. The fellow looked harmless enough, but it was best not to take chances.
5. The man claimed to have a message of some importance.

Identify the gerunds; bracket their phrases. Give their functions: S, O, SC, OP. Punctuate as needed.

6. Seeing the man with no obvious weapons calmed the knight a bit.
7. His captain was a worry wart when it came to warning him but it seemed foolish to think a mere peasant could do him any real harm.
8. The knight was careful to check and see if he was out of bow range from the nearby woods.
9. Arrows had a way of penetrating armor and these local archers had no love for the knights in his group.
10. The knight was smiling to himself as he reached for his sword in order to take the offered scroll of paper from the peasant.

Create sentences of your own that fit the parameters described below.

11. gerund as subject
12. gerund phrase as subject
13. gerund as object preposition
14. gerund as direct object
15. gerund as subject complement

Write sentences that fit the formulas below; tie them together into a single story or description.

16. S Rp V O Inf-mod.

17. Sub S V O S V Pp.

18. Inf-S V O c/c S V O Rp.

19. S Rp V O c/a S V O.

20. Pp Pp S V O S V Pp.

Since the gerund functions as a noun, the gerund phrase may be a bit different from the infinitive and the participial phrases. The difference is that **the gerund phrase may begin with a word other than a gerund.**

The reason this can and does occur is precisely because the gerund is acting as a noun; it has modifiers. The words that might start a gerund phrase are usually noun markers (NM) or perhaps an adjective.

> ☞ *Running around the track* was a big deal.
> ☞ *His running around the track* was a big deal.
> ☞ *Quickly running around the track* was a big deal.

In first example above the gerund phrase begins with the gerund. In the second example, however, a noun marker, *his*, precedes the gerund. It is included in the phrase since it modifies the gerund itself. Be careful to look to the left of gerund a word or two to see if those words modify the gerund and are naturally associated with the gerund. If so, such words must be included in the gerund phrase.

Below are a series of examples of gerund phrases used in various ways. The gerund phrases are in italic print.

> ☞ *Wading through the swollen river* was a dangerous ordeal.
> ☞ *The generous giving of the congregation* came to an abrupt halt.
> ☞ A prime Elizabethan sport was *the baiting of bulls and bears*.
> ☞ Jerry's idea of fun was *wasting a day in front of the TV set*.
> ☞ Even the natives enjoyed *rafting down the river in the sun*.
> ☞ The gourmand especially liked *the eating of the homemade pies*.
> ☞ Francis hoped to spend a day of *resting in his hammock*.
> ☞ The policeman threw a look at *the gathering of young toughs*.

The above examples are paired to show both a gerund beginning a phrase and a phrase beginning with some word other than a gerund. Each of the four functions of nouns that gerunds can perform are represented.

Remember to look to the left of the gerund construction to find out what its function is in the sentence. Look for verbs, action or linking, or prepositions.

Action verb	=	O, direct object
Linking verb	=	SC, subject complement
Preposition	=	OP, object preposition
none of the above	=	S, subject

Gerunds 3: Phrases

For each of the following, identify the nouns and the pronouns acting as nouns and their specific functions.

1. Lord British watched as the traveler approached his throne.
2. The man was queerly dressed and had a look of much road dust on him.
3. The man approached slowly and with reverence and dignity.
4. The name that he gave was Starkling, but the name was unknown here.
5. The traveler said that he had come a great distance to see the king.

Identify the gerunds; bracket their phrases, and give their functions: S, O, SC, OP. Punctuate as needed.

6. Many of the court were watching from their positions of vantage.
7. The traveler stood before Lord British and began telling a tale of persecution and woe in a far land.
8. Lord British was listening intently as Starkling drew a grim picture of suffering and anguish in the realm beyond the mountains.
9. All who heard the traveler murmured at the tale and vowed to begin preparing for a mission of battle and mercy to the far land.
10. The king was thinking to himself and then he clapped for attention and started issuing orders to selected men in the great hall.

Create sentences of your own that fit the parameters described below.

11. gerund as subject
12. gerund phrase as subject
13. gerund phrase as object preposition
14. gerund as direct object
15. gerund phrase as direct object

Write sentences that fit the formulas below; tie them together into a single story or description.

16. S V O c/c S V O Inf-Mod.

17. S V Ger-O S c/a V Pp Pp.

18. Inf-S LV SC sub S V O Rp.

19. Sub S Rp V O S V O Pp.

20. Pp Pp S V O Pp S V Pp.

Gerund constructions are similar to infinitives in that they can occur in compound relationships and can also be either part of another verbal construction or include another verbal construction within themselves.

Compound relationships are really quite simple; two gerunds are used together in such a way that they are both of equal value. For instance, both could be used as parts of a compound subject or object.

    ☞   *Jumping* and *running* were his favorite activities.
    ☞   He liked *eating tacos* and *drinking lemonade*.

☞ Note that **the two gerund constructions in each sentence are parallel; that is, they have the same function.** In the first sentence both are subjects; in the second sentence, both are objects. As an aside, it should be noted that two unlike verbals should not be used in parallel. For instance, it would not do to use a gerund for one part of a compound subject and an infinitive for the other part.

    ☞   He liked throwing the ball and to catch it.

The above example should be rewritten to contain either two infinitive objects or two gerund objects.

    ☞   He liked throwing the ball and catching it.
    ☞   He liked to throw the ball and (to) catch it.

The second item of concern here is with a gerund construction found within another verbal construction. One such situation arises an infinitive construction uses the gerund construction as its object.

    ☞   The man began to enjoy sleeping in the hammock on the porch.

The entire infinitive construction is the object of the main verb *began*, but the gerund construction, *sleeping ... porch*, is the object of the infinitive. Proper identification of the two constructions would require double brackets.

    ☞   [to enjoy [sleeping in the hammock on the porch]]

Gerund constructions can also contain infinitive constructions.

    ☞   Trying to eat the pie in one bite was foolish.

Here the entire gerund, *trying to eat the pie in one bite*, acts as the subject, but the gerund has an object, and its object is the infinitive phrase, *to eat the pie in one bite*.

Gerunds within gerunds are also possible but are not found very often.

    ☞   Thinking about dancing with her beau consumed much of her time.

The gerund subject construction contains a gerund phrase acting as an object of the preposition. Other possibilities exist; stretch your mind and think of a few for yourself.

For each of the following, identify the nouns and the pronouns acting as nouns and their specific functions.

1. The falcon hovered in the sky as she watched the field below.
2. She was looking for something to eat and hoped to find it soon.
3. Many field mice and other critters lived in the grassy field.
4. It would be a matter of time before something edible showed up.
5. The falcon's eyes swept back and forth as she searched for prey.

Identify the infinitives and gerunds; bracket their phrases and give their functions. Punctuate as needed.

6. A mouse began thinking about the seeds of the wild oat plant.
7. His hunger began to make him forget caution so he darted forward.
8. The falcon saw the movement and in a flash was swooping down to catch the unwary mouse who was intent on eating the wild oats.
9. The falcon's claws extended wide to make a good strike on the mouse.
10. To get a good hold the falcon began gripping tightly right behind the mouse's head then she flew to a perch on a limb and rested.

Create sentences of your own that fit the parameters given below.

11. ger-subject, inf-mod ending sentence
12. inf-subject including gerund construction
13. ger-object including second ger-obj prep
14. inf-mod including gerund construction
15. ger-subject including inf-object

Write sentences that fit the formulas below; tie them together into a single story or description.

16. Pp Pp S V O c/c S Appos V O.

17. S V O Rp S V O c/a.

18. S V Pp Pp sub S V O Pp.

19. S Rp V O S c/a V O Rp.

20. Sub S V O S V Pp Pp.

Lesson 63   <u>Gerunds 5: Summation</u>

1) Gerunds are -ING forms of a verb that substitute for nouns.

2) Gerund constructions are typical verbals in that they can have words associated with them such as noun markers in front and nouns, adverbs, and prepositional phrases behind them. The words following the gerund generally answer the questions **who, what, where, when,** and **how**.

3) Gerunds usually function as subjects (S), objects (O), object prepositions (OP), or subject complements (SC).

4) Gerunds cannot be thrown out of a sentence because the sentence would lose meaning.

5) Under normal circumstances gerunds will not be separated from the rest of the sentence by punctuation. Certain punctuation situations might exist, to wit, three or more gerunds in series.

      ☞   *Jumping, vaulting* and *running* were his three best events.

6) Gerund constructions may occur in other verbal construction or may have other verbal constructions within them. Also a gerund construction can have another gerund construction within itself.

7) To find the function of a gerund construction, look to the left.
    a) preposition = OP, object preposition
    b) active verb = O, object
    c) linking verb = be careful: SC, subject complement perhaps
    d) none of the above = S, subject

8) Test to see if a *BE* form before an *-ING* form is a linking verb or a helping verb. This is done by combining the *BE* form with the *-ING* form to make one verb. If the new verb fits into the sentence well, the *-ING* form is a main verb and not a gerund. If the new verb does not fit well, then the *-ING* form is probably a gerund subject complement.

      ☞   The dog was running in the field.
      ☞   The dog ran in the field.   OK - *Running* is the main verb.

      ☞   His hobby was collecting stamps.
      ☞   His hobby collected stamps.   NO - *Collecting* is a gerund SC.

Gerunds 5: Summation

For each of the following, identify the nouns and the pronouns acting as nouns and their specific functions.

1. Rowdy Tuttle was a cowboy with some time and experience on his side.
2. He looked at the scene below him in the valley.
3. A big drive was in process with many cows and cowboys in sight.
4. Rowdy studied the situation and gave it careful thought.
5. The Bar-X boys had little love for him, and he knew it.

Identify the infinitives and gerunds; bracket their phrases and give their functions. Punctuate as needed.

6. Rowdy began talking to his horse about the possibilities.
7. He could just ride down and try to take his chances with that crowd.
8. The men were working and would not have much time to deal with him right now but evening was closing in fast and then trouble would come.
9. Turning around and riding away was another option as well.
10. Making the right decision was not easy however Rowdy decided to head down to the valley.

Create sentences of your own that fit the parameters given below.

11. inf-mod starting sentence, ger-object
12. inf-object including gerund construction
13. ger-subject including second ger-obj prep
14. ger-subject including infinitive construction
15. inf-subject, ger-subject complement

Write sentences that fit the formulas below; tie them together into a single story or description.

16. Pp S V O c/c S V O Rp.

17. S V O Pp S V O c/a.

18. S Appos V O sub S V Pp Pp.

19. Sub S Rp V O S c/a V O.

20. S V O S V O Inf-Mod.

```
┌─────────────────────────────────────────────────────────────────────┐
│                             DEFINITION                                │
│                                                                       │
│  PARTICIPLE = an -ING or -EN form of a verb used as a modifier        │
└─────────────────────────────────────────────────────────────────────┘
```

The participle is a third verbal; like the infinitive and gerund, it **is a word that retains some of its verb characteristics while it does another job, in this case one of modification.** An accurate description or definition of a participle is an *-ING* or *-EN* form of a verb used as a modifier.

Participles are simple in function in that they only do one thing, modify. Unfortunately, **participles are not always easy to spot, and that is because the *-EN* forms are quite varied in their appearance.** For this lesson only, the participles will be limited to the *-ING* variety.

Eliminating the possibilities found in *-ING* words is really just the same as for gerunds (see Lesson 59). **The first step** is to simply **toss aside those words that happen to end in *-ING* but are not actually the *-ING* forms of a verb.** The test is to cut off the *-ING* from the rest of the word and see if a decent base verb is left. Again, these spelling likenesses are rarely any trouble.

The second step is to **see if the *-ING* form is functioning as a true verb in the sentence.** To do this, it is necessary to look to the left and see if a form of *BE* is present. If a *BE* form exists, attempt to combine it with the *-ING* form. If they combine and make sense in the sentence, the *-ING* form is a main verb. If the combination is not good, then the *-ING* form is a verbal.

At this point it is necessary to decide if the verbal has other words connected with it. Once again the method is to ask the questions **who, what, where, when,** and **why.** After determining the phrase, the next step is to try and throw the verbal construction out of the sentence. If the construction can be thrown out without altering the basic meaning of the sentence, it will be a participle.

Note that **the distinctive between the participle and the gerund** is that **one is a modifier** while **the other is a noun substitute.** The same test that tells the function in infinitives is used to differentiate between participles and gerunds. Noun substitutes cannot be thrown out while modifiers can.

☞   His idea of fun is *running in the snow.*
☞   He watched the dog *running in the snow.*

The phrase under consideration is *running in the snow.* **The test is to throw it out of the sentences.** In the first example sentence, the phrase cannot be dropped without distorting the sentence; the phrase is a gerund. In the second sentence, however, the phrase can easily be left out; it is a participle modifier.

When found in the *-ING* form, both the participle and gerund look exactly the same. **The key to discerning participles and gerunds is by their function; modifiers can be dropped while noun substitutes cannot.**

For each of the following, identify the nouns and the pronouns acting as nouns and their specific functions.

1. Glaucus hauled on the rope with great strength as it came from the deep.
2. The fisherman worked tirelessly at the nets almost continuously.
3. When the edge of the net appeared, Glaucus leaned over for a look.
4. He was looking for fish, and he hoped to see many of them.
5. The net seemed heavier this time, so he was quite hopeful.

Identify the verbals; bracket their phrases, and identify their type and function. Punctuate as needed.

6. Looking over the side was a bit dangerous for the fisherman.
7. One little slip and he would be pulled over the side and he would be caught swimming in his own net.
8. Glaucus smiled to himself as he saw many fins breaking the water.
9. It would be a good catch but now he had to haul with all his might to get the net up then he could start counting his catch.
10. The rope groaned in the pulley but Glaucus pulled harder and in moments the net was resting on the deck with fish flopping in it.

Create sentences of your own that fit the parameters given below.

11. ger-subject, inf-modifier ending sentence
12. participle modifying the object
13. ger-object including second ger-obj prep
14. participle modifying the subject
15. inf-modifier starting sentence, ger-subject

Write sentences that fit the formulas below; tie them together into a single story or description.

16. Pp S V O c/c S Appos V O.

17. S V Pp S V O c/a.

18. S Pp Pp V O sub S V Pp Pp.

19. S V O S c/a V O Rp.

20. Inf-Mod S V O S V O Pp.

The participle comes in two basic forms, the **-ING form which always ends in -ING, and the -EN form which comes in many varied endings.** The -ING form is commonly referred to as the present participle. The -EN form is called the past participle. One helpful feature for determining the -EN form is to see if it fits into the verb form test frame *I have _____.* You should have learned this from the chart in the first book.

It is helpful to be reminded again that the -EN form has some regularity. If a verb is a regular verb, the -EN form will end in -ED. If the verb is an irregular verb, however, the -ING form will also be irregular. Irregular verbs do form families which act similarly to others in the same family.

    ☞   driven, ridden, written
    ☞   brought, fought, caught
    ☞   sung, rung, swung
    ☞   found, bound, ground
    ☞   drunk, stunk, shrunk

To make the -EN form, some verbs add other letters; some change internally, and some do nothing at all. **The best defense for checking if a verb is in the -EN form is to use the test frame, *I have _____.***

The job of deciding whether the -EN form is functioning as a main verb or a participle is accomplished by looking to the left. If a form of *HAVE* is just to the left of the -EN form, the -EN form is probably a main verb. **A second check is to combine the *HAVE* form with the -EN form to make one verb.** If that verb fits into the sentence without changing meaning, the -EN form is certainly the main verb. Combining the -EN form with *HAVE* is very like combining the -ING form with *BE*; the same principles apply.

    ☞   The dog *has eaten* its food.
    ☞   The dog *ate* its food.

In the example note that the verb *eaten* is preceded by a form of *HAVE* and that they will readily combine into one verb that makes sense. Obviously, *eaten* is the main verb in the sentence.

When no *HAVE* form precedes the -EN form, the -EN form is then a participle.

    ☞   The dog ate the *burned* chops.
    ☞   The dog ate the chops *left on the table*.

Remember that the participle has only one function; it modifies. Because it modifies, it can be dropped from the sentence. A main verb cannot be dropped from the sentence without the meaning being changed.

    ☞   The dog has eaten its food.   The dog has its food.
    ☞   The dog ate the burned chops.   The dog ate the chops.

Note that in the first sentence when the verb is dropped, the sentence changes meaning. In the second example sentence the meaning is quite the same without the participle.

Participles 2: *-EN* Forms **Exercise 65**

For each of the italicized words give its specific function. Also punctuate as needed.

1. Armstrong the boy *wonder* rode the *horse* with agility and *grace*.
2. The *crowd* in the main *tent* watched with *amazement* at the stunts.
3. They applauded his *finesse* and *they* loved his *showmanship*.
4. *Armstrong* put the *horse* through many intricate *maneuvers*.
5. The whole *act* went quickly however the *crowd* was quite satisfied.

Identify the verbals; bracket their phrases, and identify their type and function. Punctuate as needed.

6. Running into the bigtop next was a silly fellow dressed in yellow.
7. It was obvious that he was a clown because he started to fall over his own feet but then three others came in hopping and jumping.
8. The crowd laughed as they saw the clowns falling over one another.
9. Armstrong was a tough act to follow but the clowns were very good in fact the crowd began to applaud them for their rollicking antics.
10. The polished look of Armstrongs performance was quite the opposite of the apparent haphazard clowning of the four actors now in the ring.

Fill in the [ ] with the construction asked for; punctuate if needed.

11. [Ger-S] was what he wanted to do.
12. He took a shot at the [part] partridge.
13. [Inf-Mod] the dog went into the grass.
14. The small [part] dog darted under the fence.
15. Everyone hoped [inf-O [ger-OP]].

Write sentences that fit the formulas below; tie them together into a single story or description.

16. Pp S Rp V O c/c S V O Pp.

17. S Appos V Pp S V O c/a.

18. Sub S Part V O S V Pp Pp.

19. Pp Pp Pp S V O sub S V O.

20. Inf-Mod S V Pp S V O Pp.

Lesson 66   Participles 3: Punctuation & Placement

The participial modifier either occurs as a single word or has a phrase associated with it. It is helpful to know the rule for modifiers and the punctuation associated with them. That is the focus of this lesson.

Placement rule: A **single word modifier precedes** the word it modifies while a **phrase modifier generally follows** the word it modifies.

    ☞   The *driving* rain fell all night long.
    ☞   The rain *driving in the from the east* fell all night long.

In the above examples the participial modifiers are in italics. Note that the **single word modifier** in the first sentence comes **before** the word it modifies. In the second example the **phrase modifier follows** the word it modifies.

Two items should be noted here. **First**, the placement rule is common to other modifiers of nouns in English and is not limited to participles. For instance, adjectives most often precede the nouns they modify while prepositional phrases generally tag along after the nouns they modify. **Second**, sentence modifiers do not function in quite the same way as noun modifiers do.

There is an exception to the placement rule. This occurs in the subject only, and it occurs with the phrase. Sometimes the phrase that modifies the subject can be placed before the subject. It can also be placed in its normal position behind the subject as well.

    ☞   Running from the bear, the girl screamed for help.
    ☞   The girl running from the bear screamed for help.

Punctuation Rule: When a verbal modifier begins a sentence, it is set off from the rest of the sentence by a comma. Note that the verbal can be a participle or an infinitive.

    ☞   Floundering around in the water, the man grabbed for the preserver.
    ☞   To get a good hold of it, the man crooked it in his arm.
    ☞   Worn out from his struggle, the man hung limply in the preserver.

A second possible use of punctuation with participial modifiers occurs when the phrase follows a very specific noun that is identifiable without the modifier. In such a case, commas could separate the participial modifier as being non-essential to the sentence. It is much that same as the commas used for relative clauses when they follow a specific noun.

    ☞   The dog eating his food kept his ears on the alert.
    ☞   Bruno, eating his food, kept his ears on the alert.
    ☞   The dog that was eating his food kept his ears on the alert.
    ☞   Bruno, who was eating his food, kept his ears on the alert.

Participles 3: Punctuation & Placement   Exercise 66

For each of the italicized words give its specific function. Also punctuate as needed.

1. The *farmer* strode off through his *field* toward the lower forty *acres*.
2. His *gun* was on his *shoulder* as he disappeared into the *hollow*.
3. The gophers in the *field* would feel the *bite* of *bullets* today.
4. The farmers *patience* was gone so he wanted *blood* and *bounties*.
5. A box of *shells* filled his *pockets* for the expected good *hunting*.

Identify the verbals; bracket their phrases, and identify their type and function. Punctuate as needed.

6. Creeping over the hilltop the farmer looked carefully for movement.
7. The gophers would move their heads or tails and this slight movement was enough to give the farmer an exact location of a gopher.
8. The farmer quickly spotted two running gophers on the far side.
9. They slipped into their holes so no shot was possible however the farmer did not have long to wait soon he saw a head turning around.
10. The astonished gopher jumped as the shot erupted dirt at his feet the gopher however fell into his hole while the fuming farmer reloaded.

Fill in the [ ] with the construction asked for; punctuate if needed.

11. [Ger-S] is the best treat of all.
12. Brisco enjoyed the [part] ice cream cone.
13. The heat was melting the ice cream [part].
14. A small [part] dog waited at the edge of the table.
15. He obviously wanted [inf-O [ger-OP]].

Write sentences that fit the formulas below; tie them together into a single story or description.

16. Part S V O c/c S V O Pp Pp.

17. Sub S V S V O Inf-Mod.

18. Pp Pp S Part V O S V Pp.

19. Pp S Rp V O sub S V O.

20. S Part V Pp S V Part O Pp.

Lesson 67 Participles 4: Generation

Where do participial modifiers come from? **Participial modifiers come from other sentences.** Participle generation is similar to relative clause generation. There is a source sentence from which to extract the idea, in this case a participial modifier. There is also a consumer sentence with a related item to which the modifier will become attached.

     ☞   A (source): The dog was barking at the cat.
     ☞   B (consumer): The dog was under the house.
     ☞   Single Part of A; place in B.
     ☞   (result): The *barking* dog was under the house.

     ☞   Part phrase of A; place in B.
     ☞   (result): The dog *barking at the cat* was under the house.
     ☞   (alternate): *Barking at the cat*, the dog was under the house.

In most cases the participle generated can be either a single word or a phrase. The source sentence is the limiting factor. If anything follows the verb in the source sentence, some of it will usually be included in the new participial phrase. When the participial phrase is placed in a sentence to modify the subject, it is best to try both ways to see which one reads the best. In the example above the phrase modifier following the subject reads better than the alternate construction even though both are technically correct. It is a matter of sense and style.

The process of extracting the participle from the source sentence is simply to find the *-ING* or *-EN* verb form which can be utilized and then remove it, along with its phrase if desired, to the proper position in the consumer sentence in relation to the related item.

One further point needs to made. In some sentences no apparent participle form of a verb is evident. This usually can be remedied in active verb sentences by making the source sentence passive. Making it passive will always produce an *-EN* form verb which is the past participle.

     ☞   A. The ball broke the window.
     ☞   B. The man looked at his window.
     ☞   Single Part of A; place in B.
     ☞   (make A passive) The window was broken by the ball.
     ☞   (result): The man looked at his broken window.
     ☞   Part phrase of A; place in B.
     ☞   (result): The man looked at his window broken by the ball.

From the above it should be evident the generation of a participle is nothing to fear. Simply search the source sentence for an *-ING* or *-EN* form of a main verb or create and *-EN* form by making the sentence passive.

For each of the italicized words give its specific function. Also punctuate as needed.

1. *Alphonse* stroked the bears *head* as he looked through the *bushes*.
2. The *men* on the road were from the *city* and were looking for *him*.
3. Alphonse had put on a show in the *town* but *he* didnt get a *license*.
4. The *town* fathers were upset about not getting their *money* for *fees*.
5. The *bear* growled deep in his *throat* and the men turned in their *tracks*.

Identify the verbals; bracket their phrases, and give their type and function. Punctuate as needed.

6. Making as little noise as possible Alphonse moved backwards.
7. The searching men were moving in his direction and he hoped to avoid them but he thought it would be tough going to get away.
8. One of the townsmen saw some moving brush off to the left and yelled.
9. The men turned in that direction and stumbled into the forest so Alphonse and the bear hustled across the winding road to safety.
10. The searchers soon gave up the chase and began heading back towards town Alphonse however was on his way down the forsaken road.

A. Alphonse had the bear on a leash.
B. Alphonse was a good trainer.
C. The bear was dancing a jig.
D. The people watched the bear.

11. Sub C; place before D.
12. Appos of B; place in A.
13. Passive of D; Rp of D; place in C.
14. Rp of B; Rp of C; place in A.
15. Single Part of C; place in D.

Write sentences that fit the formulas below; tie them together into a single story or description.

16. S V O Part c/a S V O Pp.

17. Part S V S V O Rp.

18. Pp Pp S Part V O S V O Inf-Mod.

19. Part S Rp V O sub S V Part O.

20. Sub S V Pp S V O Part.

Lesson 68   Participles 5: Compounds & Inserts

Participle constructions are similar to other verbals in that they **can occur in compound relationships** and **can also be either part of another verbal construction or include another verbal construction within themselves.**

The **first** compbination is a **compound relationship**; it does not occur very often since modifiers don't often occur in equal pairs. Two examples are given below. Two single participles are treated as coordinate adjectives and separated by a comma; two participial phrases would generally require a coordinating conjunction.

     ☞   The *jumping*, *running* dog was a favorite performer.
     ☞   *Looking around the corner* and *sneaking into the alley*, the detective carefully made his way.

The **second** type of combination is where a **participle construction is found within another verbal construction.** The usual combination is a single participle modifying a noun in a gerund or infinitive phrase.

     ☞   The man enjoyed sleeping in the *swinging* hammock on the porch.
     ☞   To run by the *panting* competition was a real joy.

The two constructions above each have a single word participle modifying a noun within the verbal phrase. Each participle could be removed from the verbal phrase without harming the essential meaning of the phrase.

Participial constructions can also contain other verbal constructions, but they are not common. See the examples below.

     ☞   Trying to eat the pie in one bite, the boy looked quite foolish.
     ☞   Hearing the warning over the radio, the soldier ducked his head.

In the first example the participle contains an infinitive phrase [part [inf-O]]; the second example uses a gerund within the participle [part [ger-O]].

Participles within participles are also possible but are not found very often.

     ☞   Thinking about his dancing dog, the trainer left the tent.

Many combinations are possible. It is informative to try all possible combinations. Working out formulas and examples to fit would be good exercise. Below are a few to try.

        [part [inf [ger]]]
        [inf [ger including part]]
        [part [ger including part]]

For each of the italicized words, give its specific function. Also punctuate as needed.

1. The *gunman* hovered over the *visiplate* as he watched the alien *fighter*.
2. The *alien* was coming in with unclear *intentions* and *designs*.
3. The commander of the WPU *ship* gave no *order* to fire at the *alien*.
4. It would be a short *time* before the *home* ship lost its *advantage*.
5. Suddenly a *port* opened on the alien *vessel* as she banked to the *right*.

Identify the verbals; bracket their phrases, and give their type and function. Punctuate as needed.

6. The gunner began wondering about what defense shields the alien had.
7. Attempting radio contact the commander tried many channels.
8. The alien made no menacing actions but began moving closer.
9. Shifting into a good firing position the gunner waited out the drama.
10. To make their intentions known the aliens put out a white flag.

A. The alien craft was fast and sleek.
B. The gunner was a crack shot.
C. The gunner was watching the alien.

11. Sub A; place before C.
12. Rp of A; place in C.
13. Appos of B; place in C.
14. Single word part of C; place in B.
15. Part phrase of C; place in B.

Write sentences that fit the formulas below; tie them together into a single story or description.

16. Part S V O c/c S Appos V O.

17. S V O Rp S V O c/a.

18. S V Pp sub S V O Inf-Mod.

19. S Rp V O S c/a V O Rp.

20. Sub S V O S V O Part.

1) Participles are *-ING* forms or *-EN* forms of a verb that are used as modifiers.

2) Participle constructions are typical verbals in that they can have words associated with them such as noun markers in front and nouns, adverbs, and prepositional phrases behind them. Those words following the participle that are part of the participial phrase generally answer the questions **who, what, where, when,** and **how**.

3) Participles have only one function; they modify.

4) Because participles modify, they can always be thrown out of the sentence. The sentence will still make sense and have acceptable grammar although some loss in meaning may occur.

5) Single word participial modifiers precede the word they modify.

    ☞   The *running* dog ducked under the fence.

6) Participial phrase modifiers usually follow the word they modify.

    ☞   The dog *running through the field* ducked under the fence.

7) Sometimes the participial phrase will modify the subject and start the sentence. In this case, it is an introductory verbal modifier and should be set off from the rest of the sentence by a comma.

    ☞   *Looking around the corner*, the detective stepped into the alley.

8) Participial constructions can occur in other verbal constructions or may have other verbal constructions within them. Participles may also occur within other participial constructions.

    ☞   The man enjoyed painting the *rusted* plow.
    ☞   To drink the *cooling* liquid was a treat.
    ☞   *Hoping to find the quarter*, the man searched on his hands and knees.
    ☞   *Thinking about eating a pizza*, the boy headed for lunch.
    ☞   *Seeing the flashing light*, the driver slowed down.

9) The *-ING* forms always end in *-ING*.

10) The *-EN* forms will fit into the test frame: "I have _____."

11) A phrase modifier following a specific or easily identifiable noun will have commas around it. Conversely, a phrase modifier following a general noun will not have commas.

    ☞   Bill, *watching the forklift*, didn't hear his mom call.
    ☞   The boy *watching the forklift* didn't hear his mom call.

12) Participles are generated as modifiers by either lifting the *-ING* or *-EN* forms from the source sentence or by creating an *-EN* form by making the source sentence passive.

    ☞   (source) The dog was running in the field.
    ☞   thus: the running dog   or: the dog running in the field

Participles 6: Summation

For each of the italicized words, give its specific function. Also punctuate as needed.

1. The *outlaw* looked over the *sights* of his Spencer *rifle*.
2. The intended *victim* was riding along the *path* without any *suspicions*.
3. The man waiting in the *trees* gave no *hint* of his *presence*.
4. It was almost the right *time* to shoot the *man* and get his *poke*.
5. Suddenly a *bird* flew up and the *rider* veered off the *trail*.

Identify the verbals; bracket their phrases, and give their type and function. Punctuate as needed.

6. The disappointed outlaw began watching the brush very carefully.
7. Attempting to get a good shot off the trail would be quite risky.
8. The outlaw decided to wait for the vanished rider.
9. Getting down from his horse the outlaw rested his gun on a log.
10. The horse standing by him was a good mustang and it waited quietly.

A. The outlaw was watching the brush near the trail.
B. The brush was good cover.
C. The outlaw was pointing his gun down the trail.

11. Sub A; place before C.
12. Rp of C; place in A.
13. Appos of B; place in A.
14. Single word part of A; place in C.
15. Part phrase of C; place in A.

Write sentences that fit the formulas below; tie them together into a single story or description.

16. S Part V O c/a S V O Pp.

17. S Rp V O sub S V O.

18. Inf-Mod S V Pp S V O Pp.

19. S V O Pp c/c S V O Rp.

20. Sub S V O Part S V O.

1. look for infinitives: *to + verb*
- a. beware of *to* as a preposition (*to* + nonverb)
- b. decide phrase if any (who, what, where, when, how)
- c. attempt to throw it out of the sentence
    - 1) yes, makes sense without it = modifier
    - 2) no = noun substitute (now look to the left)
        - a) active verb = O, object
        - b) linking verb = SC, subject complement (or PN)
        - c) neither of the above = S, subject

2. look for -*ING* words
- a. eliminate the -*ING* spelling likenesses (*thing, evening, sing* and so forth)
- b. determine if main verb (Is a *BE* form in front? Will it combine?)
    - ☞   is running = runs ??
- c. decide phrase if any (who, what, where, when, how)
- d. attempt to throw it out
    - 1) yes = modifier = participle
    - 2) no = noun substitute = gerund (now look to the left)
        - a) preposition = OP, object preposition
        - b) active verb = O, object
        - c) linking verb = SC, subject complement (or PN)
        - d) none of the above = S, subject

3. look for an -*EN* form
- a. decide phrase if any (who, what, where, when, how)
- b. attempt to throw it out - if yes = modifier = participle

4. brief descriptions of noun functions
- a. SUBJECT: who or what is doing or being in the sentence, who or what the sentence is talking about   ☞ *Oscar* went home.
- b. OBJECT: who or what receives the action of the verb, who or what is being acted upon by the subject   ☞ Oscar shot the *bear.*
- c. SUBJECT COMPLEMENT: a renaming of the subject, a second noun connected by a linking verb which equals the subject   ☞ Oscar is a good *boy.*
- d. OBJECT PREPOSITION: answers who or what for the preposition   ☞ in the *field*
- e. INDIRECT OBJECT: who or what gets the object, correct order is giver (S), getter (IO), gift (O)   ☞ Oscar gave *Hazel* a flower.
- f. MODIFIER: one noun describes another that immediately follows it   ☞ the *brick* house

---

VERBAL FUNCTION CHART

1. **INFINITIVE** functions = **Mod, S, O, SC**
2. **GERUND** functions = **S, O, OP, SC**
3. **PARTICIPLE** function = **Mod**

For each of the italicized words, give its specific function. Also punctuate as needed.

1. Conrad set the *trap* with care this *predator* had killed much *stock*.
2. *It* appeared to be a *coyote* but the *evidence* was scanty.
3. The man baited the *trap* with *scent* of a female *coyote*.
4. He covered the *trap* and strewed some *grass* about the *area*.
5. He gave the *trap* a final *look* and went off down the *trail*.

Identify the verbals; bracket their phrases, and give their type and function. Punctuate as needed.

6. Some time later a wandering skunk approached the hidden trap.
7. Smelling the coyote scent the skunk went to opposite edge of the trail.
8. The skunk figured to avoid trouble by staying clear of hazards.
9. Coming down a hillside a coyote sniffed the air for information.
10. The trap waiting for him sent forth its beckoning aroma.

A. The coyote was a prime specimen with thick fur.
B. The coyote was looking for a female.
C. The trap waited patiently for the coyote.

11. Coor A and B.
12. Rp of C; place in B.
13. Appos of A; place in B.
14. Single word part of B; place in A.
15. Part phrase of B; place in C.

Write sentences that fit the formulas below; tie them together into a single story or description.

16. Pp Pp S V O c/a S V Pp Pp.

17. Part S V O c/c S V O.

18. S V Pp S V O Inf-Mod

19. S V O Pp sub S LV SC Rp

20. Sub S Part V O S V O

Lesson 71

INFINITIVE: a *to* + verb combination which either 1) substitutes for a noun or
2) modifies some part of the sentence

GERUND: an *-ING* form of a verb which substitutes for a noun

PARTICIPLE: an *-ING* or *-EN* form of a verb used as a modifier

A VERBAL is a verb which retains some qualities of a verb but does the job of an adjective or a noun. It modifies or acts as a noun substitute. All three of the types listed above are verbals.

TYPE	FORM	FUNCTION
infinitive	*to* + verb	modifier or noun substitute
gerund	*-ING*	noun substitute
participle	*-ING, -EN*	modifier

ITEMS OF GENERALLY USEFUL INFORMATION

1. Single word modifiers precede the words them modify.

2. Phrases usually directly follow the words they modify. EXCEPTION: A phrase modifying the subject may precede the entire sentence; it will then be set off by a comma from the rest of the sentence.

3. Phrases normally begin with the verbal and continue with whatever answers the questions **who, what, where, when,** and **how.** Objects of the verbal and prepositional phrases make up most of the items found in verbal phrases.

4. Modifiers can be dropped from the sentence without impairing the grammar of the sentence. Although some meaning will be lost, the sentence will still make good sense.

5. Noun substitutes can NOT be dropped from the sentence without destroying the grammar; the sentence will usually sound incomplete when the noun substitutes are removed.

6. Noun functions where substitutes can appear are 1) Subjects, 2) Objects, 3) Objects of the Prepositions, 4) Subject Complements, and 5) Indirect Objects.

7. The *-ING* forms always end in *-ING*.

8. The *-EN* forms often do not end with *-EN* but will fit into the test frame "I have _____."

9. A phrase modifier following a specific or easily identifiable noun will have commas around it.
      ☞   John, looking for his mother, saw a fire truck.
    A phrase modifier following a general noun will not have commas.
      ☞   The boy looking for his mother saw a fire truck.

Verbal Notes

For each of the italicized words, give its specific function. Also punctuate as needed.

1. The *king* set up an *image* made of *gold* it was sixty cubits high.
2. He set *it* up on the *plain* of Dura in the *province* of Babylon.
3. The *king* sent for his *officials* to come to the *dedication* of the image.
4. These *officials* came and stood before the *image* and heard their *orders*.
5. When the *music* sounded *they* were to fall down and worship the *image*.

Identify the verbals; bracket their phrases, and give their type and function. Punctuate as needed.

6. The fiery furnace would be the plight of those not following the decree.
7. Most people hearing the music would fall down and worship the image.
8. Three Jews were accused of not following the order.
9. They were brought to the king to face charges.
10. The waiting king planned a harrowing experience in the furnace for them.

A. The king was an obstinate man with lots of power.
B. The king was plotting against his enemies.
C. Shadrach and his friends came before the king.

11. Coor A and B.
12. Rp of C; place in B.
13. Appos of A; place in B.
14. Single word Part of B; place in A.
15. Part phrase of B; place in C.

Write sentences that fit the formulas below; tie them together into a single story or description.

16. Pp S V O c/c Pp S V Pp.

17. S V O c/a Part S V O.

18. Sub S V Pp S V O.

19. S V O Pp sub S V O Rp.

20. S Part V O c/c V O.

Lesson 72   Parallelism

Parallelism is a concept that is linked to using grammatical constructions in series. There are numerous types of constructions that can be used in a series. **The parallelism rule** simply states that **the various parts of the series must all have the same construction.**

Obviously the easiest and perhaps most common series is a list of items or qualities. A list of items would consist of nouns while qualities would be adjectives. The parallelism rule says not to mix them in the same series, and most people don't because a series of single words is simple and obvious.

When the series moves beyond single word constructions into phrase constructions, people begin having difficulties unless they keep their grammar straight or have a good ear for what is correct. It is wrong to mix prepositional phrases and nouns in a series as equals.

> ☞   The boys went to the ball game, to the show, and the arcade.

The final item of the series needs the preposition to make it equal with the other items in the series. The above sentence could be rewritten two ways to be correct. Note that each way has a series of equals.

> ☞   The boys went to the ball game, to the show, and to the arcade.
> ☞   The boys went to the ball game, the show, and the arcade.

Greater sophistication comes with verbals. Verbals in a series must all be alike regarding type to be correct. A series can be three or more participles, three or more gerunds, or three or more infinitives, but the various types of verbals are not to be mixed together as equals in the same series.

> ☞   He enjoyed running, hiking, and to fish.   (wrong, non-parallel constructions)
> ☞   He enjoyed running, hiking, and fishing.   (correct, all gerunds)
> ☞   He liked to run, to hike, and to fish.   (correct, all infiinitives)

When the verbals are phrases, the same condition applies. Note the following examples carefully. They are all correct in that each series has elements that are equal to others in its group.

> ☞   To eat a big steak, to have pie for dessert, and to relax afterwards by the pool was
>   Harry's idea of a nice summer evening.
> ☞   Dragging out the ice chest, grabbing up a cold drink, and taking a long swig, the
>   man satisfied his thirst.
> ☞   Bart always enjoyed planning the trip, packing the car, and driving to the intended
>   vacation spot.

Parallelism is also a matter of style as well as correctness. In some cases making the elements of the series equal in all ways possible may produce a nice effect. Note in the following example how the second sentence seems to finish off a bit more nicely than the first.

> ☞   The fox ran through the snow, slipped under the fence, and disappeared.
> ☞   The fox ran through the snow, slipped under the fence, and disappeared into the night.

Parallelism **Exercise 72**

For each of the italicized words, give its specific function. Also punctuate as needed.

1. Hecla held the *sling* with ease as his *squad* watched the *men* below.
2. The *Persians* were coming along a *path* that afforded no *cover*.
3. The Greek put a *stone* into the *pouch* of his *sling*.
4. *He* would try to hit an *archer* first his uphill *position* helped.
5. The *squad leader* would give the *signal* any time soon.

Identify the verbals; bracket their phrases, give their type and function. Punctuate as needed.

6. Kneeling behind the rocks the five Greeks waited to spring the trap.
7. The oncoming Persians apparently suspected nothing and moved slowly.
8. The effective sling range was coming up fast so Hecla watched his leader to be instantly ready to begin the ambush.
9. Shooting and running uphill would be tough for the Persians.
10. To catch them by surprise would give the Greeks a decided advantage.

Create sentences of your own that fit the parameters given below.

11. three gerunds in a series
12. single word participle modifying the subject
13. participial phrase modifying the subject and starting the sentence
14. same as #13 but with participial phrase behind subject
15. three prepositional phrases in a series

Write sentences that fit the formulas below; tie them together into a single story or description.

16. Inf-mod S V Pp c/c S V O.

17. Part S V O c/a S V O.

18. Sub S Pp V Pp S V Pp Pp.

19. S V O Pp S V c/a O Rp.

20. S Pp V O S V Part O.

Lesson 73   <u>Internal Punctuation 3: Modifiers</u>

Modifiers of nouns in sentences may or may not be separated from the noun with punctuation. There are **three keys to understanding whether commas are used or not**. The **first key** is the **size of the modifier**. If the modifier is a single word, it will not be separated from the noun it modifies with any punctuation. Single word modifiers of nouns precede the word they modify unless they are subject complements (S LV A).

    ☞   The girl is pretty.
    ☞   The pretty girl solved the equation in record time.

The **second key** is **position**. In most instances phrase modifiers follow the noun they modify. When a phrase modifier precedes the noun it modifies, the phrase will begin the sentence and will be set off from the subject by a comma. You have seen this (Lesson 66) with introductory participial phrases.

    ☞   Concentrating on the target, the shooter took careful aim.

So far, so good. **When the phrase modifier follows the word it modifies, the third key comes into play.** This is the only gray area and requires judgment on the part of the writer. **The key here is the word being modified, not the modifier itself.** If the word being modified is non-specific, then the modifier is necessary, and no punctuation is required. If the word being modified is specific and identifiable, then the modifier is not necessary and needs separation. You will note that proper nouns are very specific.

    ☞   The shooter concentrating on the target took careful aim.
    ☞   Cora, concentrating on the target, took careful aim.

Two sets of names appear in grammar that describe modifiers of this nature: essential and nonessential, and restrictive and nonrestrictive. The first label of each pair means that the modifier is needed and will not have punctuation. The last label of each pair means the modifier is not needed to identify the noun being modified and is thus an extra and should be separated from the rest of the sentence with one or two commas depending on where the modifier occurs.

What kinds of modifiers fall into these categories? Fortunately there are **only two, relative patterns** and **participial phrases**, and you have already studied both of them (Lessons 48 & 66)

    ☞   The girl who owned a horse was buying a saddle.
    ☞   Janice, who owned a horse, was buying a saddle.

    ☞   The policeman searching for the thief uncovered some clues.
    ☞   Barney Olson, searching for the thief, uncovered some clues.

    ☞   The judges picked the students dressed as Jonah and the whale.
    ☞   The judges picked Iris and Sam, dressed as Jonah and the whale.

Where do these modifiers occur? They can follow any noun in the sentence, but **generally they follow subjects, direct objects, and subject complements.** Phrase modifiers of indirect objects and objects of the preposition are rare. It is important to note that the nonessential modifiers are separated on both sides with commas if they occur within the sentence.

Internal Punctuation 3: Modifiers

For each of the italicized words, give its specific function. Also punctuate as needed.

1. Fatima smiled as the *soldiers* filed into the *room* below the *balcony*.
2. *They* were hot and tired after their long *march* and suspected *nothing*.
3. The first *job* was to feed *them* then *Fatima* would serve some wine.
4. The *officer* might object at first but *Nurad* would drug his *food*.
5. The *soldiers* were the *enemy* and this was not a friendly *town*.

Identify the verbals; bracket their phrases, and give their type and function. Punctuate as needed.

6. Gliding down the stairs Fatima smiled to the soldiers in their seats.
7. The tired men responded indifferently and waited for their food.
8. The single officer commanding this group moved toward the long bar and began to issue orders for the food to be served.
9. Nurad looking at the officer appeared to be a smiling sympathizer.
10. To snare this bunch with trickery would please him greatly.

Create sentences of your own that fit the parameters given below.

11. three prepositional phrases in a series
12. nonessential participial phrase modifying the object
13. single word participle modifying the object
14. nonessential relative pattern modifying the subject
15. three participles in a series

Write sentences that fit the formulas below; tie them together into a single story or description.

16. S V Inf-O c/c S V O.

17. S Part V O c/c Pp S V O.

18. Sub S Pp V Pp S V Pp Pp.

19. Part S V O Pp c/a S V O Rp.

20. S Pp V O c/c Part O.

Nouns and verbs are the two most active players in sentences. These two parts of speech make up most of the words in the English language and are crucial to the meaning in sentences. What follows is review.

The nouns have six functions; these functions are **determined by the relationship of the noun to other words in the sentences.** Usually we employ looking to the left to decide the function.

1. locate the noun in question
2. look to the left
    a. if a preposition is found, function = OP
    b. if an active verb is found, function = O**
    c. if a linking verb is found, function = SC
    d. if none of the above is found, probable function = S
    e. two other noun functions do exist
        1) MOD - points to another noun directly to its right
        2) IO** - comes between a *give* type verb and O

    ☞   The *enemy soldier* was a *sniper*, and he gave the *squad fits* at *night*.

In the above sentence we have all possible noun functions represented: *enemy* (MOD), *soldier* (S), *sniper* (SC), *squad* (IO), *fits* (O), and *night* (OP). Looking to the left helps identify the function. To the left of *enemy* there are no prepositions or verbs; however, *enemy* points to *soldier* on the right and modifies it. *Soldier* has no preposition or verb to its left and is modified by *enemy*; it is the subject. *Sniper* has a linking verb to its left, so it is a subject complement. *Squad* has an active verb to its left, but the verb is a *give* type; *squad* is not given by the sniper but rather receives something from the sniper; thus, it is an indirect object. *Fits* is the object; the verb to its left is active, and it tells what the sniper gave. *Night* has a preposition to its left, so it is an object of the preposition.

It is obvious that **in order to tell the function of many nouns, you must be able to identify the verbs as well.** In fact, you must be able to not only identify the verb but also decide if it is **active or linking.** Fortunately there are **only 12 common linking verbs in their various forms. Being able to recognize these few verbs on sight makes grammar much easier.**

> BE, BECOME, REMAIN
> LOOK APPEAR, TASTE, SMELL, SOUND, FEEL
> ACT, GROW, SEEM

Linking verbs require the nouns that follow them to be subject complements while **active verbs force the object role, and sometimes the indirect object role, on the nouns that follow them.**

You will also remember that noun substitutes such as **gerunds and infinitives take on one of the noun functions when they occur.** The nice thing about it all is that no noun or noun substitute can ever do more than one job at once.

Noun & Verb Functions: Review

For each of the italicized words, give its specific function. Also punctuate as needed.

1. Columbus was a *man* of great *importance* in *history*.
2. His voyage and *discovery* of *America* influenced many *events* in history.
3. Christopher was obviously used in *Gods plan* for this *world*.
4. *Christopher* whose *name* means Christ-bearer believed that *God* had called him.
5. *Some* of Christophers favorite *verses* are found in the *book* of Isaiah.

Identify the verbals; bracket their phrases, and give their type and function. Punctuate as needed.

6. Those verses speak about being called to bring light to the people from afar.
7. The learned men and rulers of the day rejected Columbus and his ideas.
8. Columbus felt that God was sending him across the seas so admitting failure at home he sought listening ears at a foreign court.
9. Father Juan Perez proved to be the man of the hour for Columbus.
10. He urged Queen Isabella to reconsider Columbus and his daring ideas.

Create sentences of your own that fit the parameters given below.

11. three gerunds in a series as subjects
12. nonessential participial phrase modifying the subject
13. essential participial phrase modifying the object
14. nonessential relative pattern modifying a subject complement
15. three participial phrases in a series

Write sentences that fit the formulas below; tie them together into a single story or description.

16. S V O Pp c/c Pp S V.

17. S V O Part c/a S V O Pp.

18. Sub S V O S V Pp Pp.

19. Inf-mod S V O c/a S V O Pp.

20. Ger-S V O c/c S V Part O.

Having now been exposed to various constructions in the English language, you should see that the extracting of one idea from a sentence and putting it into another allows for some variety in method. **There are two basic operations available** with various methods applicable in each operation.

The first general method is called addition. In this method two sentences are combined by simply adding the one sentence to the other. This was covered in the major punctuation section (Lessons 40-45). The two sentences can be coordinated, subordinated, or simply punctuated together with or without a conjunctive adverb.

The second general method is called embedding. In this method some part of the source sentence is extracted and placed or embedded into the consumer sentence. Single words, phrases, or clauses may be extracted. Here is where the choice and variety are rich. Throughout the lessons in this series, you have been forced to utilize these various methods of putting ideas together into sentences. Now you in your own writings have the opportunity to build your sentences according to your own desires and needs.

Let's look at some possibilities.

    A. The girl was swimming in the lake.
    B. The girl was dreaming about a ranch.

1. The girl swimming in the lake was dreaming about a ranch.
2. Swimming in the lake, the girl was dreaming about a ranch.
3. The swimming girl was dreaming about a ranch.
4. The girl who was swimming in the lake was dreaming about a ranch.
5. The girl was dreaming about a ranch while she was swimming in the lake.
6. The girl was dreaming about a ranch while she was swimming.
7. The girl was dreaming about a ranch while swimming.
8. The girl was dreaming about a ranch while swimming in the lake.
9. The girl, while swimming in the lake, was dreaming about a ranch.
10. The girl, while swimming, was dreaming about a ranch.
11. While swimming in the lake, the girl was dreaming about a ranch.
12. While swimming, the girl was dreaming about a ranch.
13. The girl was dreaming about a ranch and swimming in the lake.
14. The girl in the lake was dreaming about a ranch.
15. In the lake the girl was dreaming about a ranch.

In all of the above, we used B as the consumer sentence and A as the source, and not all the possibilities were shown even here. Some sentences are more precise than others. Some are longer or shorter than others. Some accentuate the additional idea while others simply include it. There are subtleties in picking the best combination for your own purposes. The language is rich and varied. You should now have a greater command of that richness and variety by virtue of the practice and familiarity gained from constructing the various combinations presented in this series of books. **May you use your ability with language to glorify God, the great Creator of all things including language.**

Structural Alternatives

For each of the italicized words, give its specific function. Also punctuate as needed.

1. At the first *Thanksgiving* the *Pilgrims* gave many *thanks* to God.
2. During that first *year many* of them had died of starvation and *sickness*.
3. With *Squantos help they* had learned to survive in the new world.
4. *They* had planted and harvested a good *crop* in their first *season*.
5. Since *God* had blessed them *they* decided to celebrate with a *feast*.

Identify the verbals; bracket their phrases, and give their type and function. Punctuate as needed.

6. They decided to invite Massasoit to have dinner with them.
7. Arriving a day early Massasoit came with 90 of his braves to dinner.
8. To come without bringing something to eat was unthinkable.
9. Having hunted along the way Massasoit brought turkeys and venison.
10. The hosting Pilgrims set a table loaded with pies and vegetables to complement the meat brought by the Indians.

Using A as the source and B as the consumer, construct different sentences using the embedding principle.

A. The dog was watching in the darkness.
B. The dog saw the thief.

11. single word participle
12. participial phrase
13. relative pattern
14. prepositional phrase
15. your choice

Write sentences that fit the formulas below; tie them together into a single story or description.

16. Ger-S LV A c/c S V Pp Pp.

17. Inf-mod S V sub S V O Part.

18. Sub S Part V O S V Pp Pp.

19. S V Part O c/a S Pp V O.

20. S V Ger-O c/c S Part V O Rp.

[See Additional Exercises, pages 182-189 for more practice.]

ADDITIONAL EXERCISES

These exercises are designed for additional practice. They can be used for improving a particular skill or for review. Normally, the extended repetition and light practice of any given skill is found in the subsequent regular exercises in the book, but at times some additional practice is desirable. These additional exercises are here for the convenience of the teacher and student in the event that a student needs some additional work on a given part of the grammar. Each teacher will make decisions about which of these exercises to use and when. All exercises below follow the order of the text; that means the exercise material is organized in a linear fashion with the subjects of the exercise loosely following the order of the materials as they are introduced in the regular exercises. For convenience, you will find a regular lesson number in brackets at the beginning of each section of these exercises. The bracketed number refers to regular lesson number which should be completed before beginning that particular set of additional exercises.

[10] Pp IDENTIFICATION #1

DIRECTIONS: Identify each of the Pp's that are in the following passage as shown in the example. You will find 26 Pp's in this exercise.

e.g. The dog chased the cat through the garden.   ANS: [through…garden]

We sat down in the boat and began to row very fast toward the other shore of the river. Above us was nothing but thick fog, and below us was the cold gray water. We rowed hard but made little progress since we had to fight a strong current. It seemed we could not reach the other bank. I hoped the fog would never lift, but a moment later my hopes came to nothing as the wind came up and in a flash our boat was without the protection of the fog. In front of us was the enemy's bank. A few yards behind us was the protecting fog.

"Go back!" I ordered, but it was too late. I heard the fire of the machine guns, and bullets whistled all around us. We jumped into the river, and at once I turned on my back and let the current carry me downstream; then I dived under. When I came up, I was in the fog again.

I began to swim very fast as the water was quite cold. Suddenly I saw something dark in front of me, so I grabbed it. It was a branch of a shrub which grew on solid ground. I climbed from the water and discovered that I was on a small island in the middle of the river.

(adapted from *Narrow is the Way* by Sergei Sazanov)

Pp IDENTIFICATION #2

DIRECTIONS: Identify each of the Pp's that are in the following passage as shown in the example. You will find 25 Pp's in this exercise.

Now, he thought. Before it's too late. The deliberate circles were narrowing steadily. He lay in the water wondering vaguely why he didn't act. There seemed to be five of them now, then six.

The undersea was darkening fast. Feeding time, he thought. They would go crazy, and it would be too late to do anything. But still he lay in the water. Deep down in him there was something that refused to die. Coward! he said angrily.

Then he was panning the gun carefully, aiming at the tiger, centering on eye. And he knew why; it was half-grown and softer-skinned than the others, and he had to cripple it. It came in close. At seven feet he let the shark have it.

There was a sound of slithering steel and a blur and a jolt. The gun leaped out of his hand, and he was gasping air through the snorkel while the shark spun around in a tight clockwise circle. It didn't pull out of it or stop but just tore on round and round like a Catherine wheel, and Mike knew he'd got it right in the eye.

The other sharks froze in the water; surprised, they hung there for a moment; then they got it. All five of them hit the tiger together, rending and snapping crazily. A great cloud of blood spread in the water.

Mike dragged himself away from the scene. It was better without the gun. He swam until he couldn't go another stroke. Then he lay out in the water, panting so hard that the mask sucked in against his face with every breath.

(adapted from "Alone in Shark Waters" by John Kruse)

Pp IDENTIFICATION #3

DIRECTIONS: Identify each of the Pp's that are in the following passage as shown in the example found in exercise #1. You will find 26 Pp's in this exercise.

I studied the map in the small bright pool of my flashlight beam. I found myself looking repeatedly at an odd little symbol near the mouth of Nankoweap Creek. As I fell asleep, lulled by the soft river sounds, I understood that I had one final chance to move back inside my museum. I left my willow thicket camp late the next day in the cool of the evening. On one sand bar, many square yards of its damp surface had been so pock marked with the fretwork of tiny feet that I could almost see the busy brown mice scurrying and scraping and nibbling in the light-footed night. On another sand bar a carp dashed away in alarm at my approach, creating a brown swirl in the tiny bay. "Ker-ploosh," and then almost at once, gliding diagonally across the current, a brown shape appeared silently. The sleek and shining little animal cruised past, then stopped beside a small mound of half-floating branches. Very slowly I moved forward and stood directly above his den. The beaver looked up at me, and in the gray dusk we both remained motionless, both plainly fascinated by what we saw.

(adapted from *The Man Who Walked Through Time* by Colin Fletcher)

Pp IDENTIFICATION #4

DIRECTIONS: Identify each of the Pp's that are in the following passage as shown in the example found in exercise #1. You will find 25 Pp's in this exercise.

Lancelot had several other adventures during his first quest, but perhaps only two are worth repeating in detail. They were both mixed up with the conservative ethics of Force Majeur. It was the old school, the Norman baronial attitude, which provided the adventures at this period, for few people can hate so bitterly and so self-righteously as the members of a ruling caste which is being dispossessed. The knights of the Round Table were sent out as a measure against Fort Mayne, and the choleric barons who lived by Fort Mayne took up the cudgels with the ferocity of despair. They would have written to *The Times* about it if there had been such a paper. The best of them convinced themselves that Arthur was newfangled and that his knights were degenerate from the standards of their fathers. The worst of them made up uglier names than Bolshevist even and allowed the brutal side of their natures to dwell on imaginary enormities which they attributed to the knights. The situation became divorced from common sense so that atrocity stories were accepted by the atrocious people. Many barons, through fear of losing their ancient powers, believed him to be a sort of poison-gas man.

(adapted from *The Once and Future King* by T.H. White)

Pp IDENTIFICATION #5

DIRECTIONS: Identify each of the Pp's that are in the following passage as shown in the example found in exercise #1. You will find 25 Pp's in this exercise.

Sir Carados had a squire to give him his spear, but Lancelot had insisted on leaving Uncle Dap at home. He had to serve himself alone. The fight was different from the one with Arthur. For one thing, the knights were more evenly matched, and in the tilt which began it, neither of them was unhorsed. They broke their ashwood spears to splinters, but both stayed in the saddle, and the horses stood the shock. In the sword-play which followed, Lancelot proved to be the better of the two. After little more than an hour's fighting, he managed to give Sir Carados such a buffet on the helm that it pierced his brain-pan. Then while the dead man was still swaying in the saddle, he caught him by the collar, pulled him under his horse's feet, dismounted in the same instant, and struck off his head. He liberated Sir Gawaine, who thanked him heartily, and rode on again into the wild ways of England without giving Carados another thought. He fell in with a young cousin of his own, Sir Lionel, and they rode together in search of wrongs to redress. But it was unwise of them to have forgotten Sir Carados.

(adapted from *The Once and Future King* by T.H. White)

Pp IDENTIFICATION #6

DIRECTIONS: Identify each of the Pp's that are in the following passage as shown in the example found in exercise #1. You will find 31 Pp's in this exercise.

By fall Mack had a job in an Omaha bank. Henry Lutz knew one of the officers well, and it was through him that Mack landed the work which consisted in part of sweeping and dusting, but which "beat plowing corn all to pieces," according to the wielder of the broom and duster.

Abbie had thought she could not stand it to see Mack leave home. All day long she had sewed shirts and mended socks for him, and all night she had stared into the dark with the worry of her boy going to the city. But with the arrival of his letters, some of her anxiety vanished. When at Christmastime he came home to spend the day, he was full of "bank talk." One would have gathered from his conversation that he was at least on the board of directors.

In the spring of '85, the day which had been set aside by the various governors for planting trees was legalized as a holiday -- and J. Sterling Morton had given Arbor Day to Nebraska, which, in turn, was eventually to give it to the other states. That summer Abbie again planned the delayed trip back home. Before she was ready, word was noised about that an academy was to open in Weeping Water in the fall.

(adapted from *A Lantern in Her Hand* by Bess Streeter Aldrich)

[12] Verb Forms

DIRECTIONS: Supply the PAST(ed) and PAST PARTICIPLE(en) forms for each verb.

1. arise	2. awake	3. bear	4. begin
5. bend	6. bid	7. bite	8. blow
9. bring	10. burst	11. buy	12. catch
13. choose	14. cling	15. come	16. creep
17. dig	18. do	19. draw	20. drink
21. drive	22. eat	23. fall	24. fight
25. flee	26. forget	27. forsake	28. freeze
29. get	30. give	31. go	32. grow
33. hang (suspend)	34. hang (execute)	35. hide	36. know
37. lay	38. learn	39. leave	40. lend
41. let	42. lie	43. lose	44. mean
45. raise	46. ride	47. ring	48. rise
49. run	50. say	51. see	52. set
53. shake	54. shoot	55. show	56. shrink
57. sing	58. sink	59. sit	60. slay
61. slide	62. slink	63. smite	64. speak
65. spin	66. spring	67. stand	68. steal
69. sting	70. stink	71. strive	72. swear
73. swim	74. swing	75. take	76. teach
77. tear	78. throw	79. tread	80. wake
81. wear	82. weave	83. win	84. wind (turn)
85. wring	86. write	87. beat	88. bind
89. break	90. find	91. fling	92. fly
93. forbid	94. grind	95. hold	96. stick
97. stride	98. strike	98. sling	100. work

[17] Ns - V Agreement #1

DIRECTIONS: Write the subject and the correct choice of verb in each sentence. Beware of the noun object of the preposition. Also write S for a singular subject and P for a plural subject.

eg. The basket of peaches (is, are) heavy.   ANS: basket = S, is

1. The gang of men (is, are) arriving for work.
2. A school of fish (swim, swims) into the net.
3. The heads of state (arrive, arrives) for the conference.
4. The team of experts (come, comes) to help them.
5. The jars of plums (is, are) on the shelf.
6. The carload of boys (was, were) on the way to the fair.
7. The herd of cattle (stampede, stampedes) down the bank.
8. A set of fractions (has, have) to be solved.
9. The string of pearls (is, are) lost.
10. A band of robbers (roam, roams) the land.
11. Some sets of tennis (last, lasts) a long time.
12. The bag of golf balls (is, are) for practice.
13. The boxes of chalk (is, are) at the chalkboard.

14. The wives of the men (wait, waits) anxiously.
15. A shipment of clothing (is, are) expected soon.
16. The plans of the man (is, are) subject to failure.
17. The clothing and hat on that model (show, shows) signs of wear.
18. An exercise on the agreement of subject and verb (help, helps) us to learn.
19. A peck of pickled peppers (was, were) left on our doorstep.
20. The collecting of stamps (take, takes) time.

Ns - V Agreement #2

DIRECTIONS: Write the subject and the correct choice of verb in each sentence. Beware of the noun object of the preposition. Also write S for a singular subject and P for a plural subject.

eg. The basket of peaches (is, are) heavy.   ANS: basket = S, is

1. One of the boys (is, are) late for the game.
2. Each of the apples (was, were) ripe.
3. Everyone (cheer, cheers) when his hero appears.
4. One of my favorite foods (is, are) spaghetti.
5. No one except Mary and Lettie (was, were) excited.
6. Neither you nor Alice (play, plays) the game correctly.
7. Each player (try, tries) to win the game.
8. One of the pies (smell, smells) burned.
9. Neither he nor she (walk, walks) to school.
10. Every boy on both teams (show, shows) good sportsmanship.
11. The man who disagrees with them (is, are) my friend.
12. Everyone of these houses (was, were) built this year.
13. Neither Mr. Jones nor Mr. Stack (earn, earns) much money.
14. Every lilac in both our yards (bloom, blooms) early.
15. There (was, were) flowers and candy given at the door.
16. Barbara and the others (hum, hums) quietly.
17. Philip and Steve (was, were) scared of the dark.
18. Jeff, along with the other scouts, (leave, leaves) today.
19. The agent with his men (was, were) checking the story.
20. The hunter with the two guides (take, takes) lots of time.

[29] Verb/Noun functions #1

DIRECTIONS: Write all main verbs & identify them as V or LV. Write each noun and give its proper function: S, O, IO, OP, Nsc (or PN), mod.

Example: A fan from the crowd was running up the aisle.
Answer: running = V; fan = S; crowd = OP; aisle = OP

1. Most of the knights had used heavy armor in battle.
2. She had deposited her money in the bank.
3. The Zulu natives are restless.
4. The new typewriter is a special model.
5. A valuable treasure lay in the remote jungle.
6. Toni gave Greg a pie for his birthday.
7. The teacher expected some expert answers from his class.
8. Many explorers seem very selective in their choice of guides.
9. The rugged cowboy rode fearlessly into the waiting bandits.
10. None of the girls in the class enjoy handling snakes.
11. The lighthouse observer was intently watching the brewing storm.
12. A brilliant flash of lightning brightened the entire sky.
13. Robin Hood easily placed his arrow in the center of the target.
14. Ruth stood at the entrance to the strange and mysterious house.
15. The heaviest rain of the year has already come.

Verb/Noun functions #2

DIRECTIONS: Write all main verbs & identify them as V or LV. Write each noun and give its proper function: S, O, IO, OP, Nsc (or PN), mod.

1. Columbus was a man of great importance in history.
2. His voyage and subsequent discovery of America have influenced all of our lives.
3. Christopher was obviously used in God's plan for this world.
4. Christopher literally means Christ-bearer.
5. To him it was a clear indication that God had called him to bring Christ to the world.
6. Some of Christopher's favorite verses were from Isaiah 49.
7. Those verses speak about missions to the people from afar.
8. The scholars and rulers of the day, however, rejected Columbus and his ideas.
9. The consensus about Columbus was that he was mad.
10. All of this treatment convinced Columbus of one thing.
11. He felt that God was sending him to Ferdinand and Isabella of Spain.
12. Columbus did not get immediate acceptance at the Spanish court.
13. He did find a sympathetic listener in Father Juan Perez.
14. Father Perez spoke with the queen in urgent words about Columbus.
15. The king and queen then sent for the adventurer with the strange ideas about the new world.

Verb/Noun functions #3

DIRECTIONS: Write all main verbs & identify them as V or LV. Write each noun and give its proper function: S, O, IO, OP, Nsc (or PN), mod.

1. At the first Thanksgiving the Pilgrims gave many thanks to God.
2. Their first year had been difficult and somewhat disastrous for most families.
3. With Squanto's help they had learned to plant, forage, and hunt.
4. They had a good harvest that first full year.
5. They decided to celebrate and invited Massasoit to have dinner with them.
6. Massasoit came with 90 of his braves to the dinner.
7. They even came a whole day early and stayed for three days total.
8. Fortunately they had hunted on the way and brought some venison and turkeys with them.
9. The Pilgrims were apprehensive but trusted to God for supply.
10. The Indians taught the Pilgrims about hoecakes and popcorn.
11. The Pilgrims prepared pies and had fruit wines for the Indians.
12. The Pilgrims also brought many of their garden vegetables to eat.
13. Both groups happily competed in shooting contests with both the gun and the bow.
14. They had foot races and wrestling games and military drills.
15. God surely blessed the Pilgrims and provided much for them to be thankful for in their adventure in the new world.

Verb/Noun functions #4

DIRECTIONS: Write all main verbs & identify them as V or LV. Write each noun and give its proper function: S, O, IO, OP, Nsc (or PN), mod.

1. The man at one of the starboard sweeps was sprawled on the deck.
2. The last heavy round of grape shot and langrage had knocked him flat.
3. Our own fore-topmast buckled with a sound of rending timber.
4. A quick rally at the long gun began almost immediately.
5. The crew of the long gun leaped with anxiety and fear to their assigned positions.
6. They dumped the shot from the pails into their guns.
7. Suddenly a long gun emerged from one of the stern ports on the *Gorgon*.
8. The *Gorgon's* stern gun bellowed old iron and bolts and pieces of kettles at us.
9. Their initial langrage barrage screamed through our sails overhead.
10. The sweating crew of our number one gun quickly fired their retort.
11. The single fourteen inch ball smashed a path through the windows of the *Gorgon*.
12. Our other long guns roared and sent a mass of white smoke and destruction flying towards the *Gorgon*.
13. A rushing noise came from within the column of smoke over the enemy.
14. The hull of the *Gorgon* split into two gaping halves.
15. Only a welter of floating planks, broken spars, and splintered fragments remained on the still, gray waters of the English Channel.

Verb/Noun functions #5

DIRECTIONS: Write all main verbs & identify them as V or LV. Write each noun and give its proper function:
S, O, IO, OP, Nsc (or PN), mod.

1. King Nebuchadnezzar made an image of gold.
2. Its height was sixty cubits, and its breadth was six cubits.
3. He set it up on the plain of Dura in the province of Babylon.
4. Then the king sent for all his officials in the provinces.
5. They were to come to the dedication of his image that he had set up.
6. These officials came and stood before the image.
7. They were then given a decree by a herald.
8. Whenever certain music sounded, it was a signal for them to act.
9. They were to fall down and worship the image.
10. Anyone who did not do so would be thrown into a fiery furnace.
11. Thereafter when people heard the music, they fell down and worshipped.
12. At least most of the people did, but a few did not comply.
13. Three Jews were accused of not following the order.
14. Enemies brought them before the king for their actions.
15. The king confronted them directly about their illegal acts.
16. Shadrach, Meshach, and Abednego had a good answer for the king.
17. They would be true to God whether He delivered them or not.
18. God could and would do what He wanted.
19. They would rather serve the true and living God instead of the king.
20. The king became very angry, so his servants threw the men into the furnace.

[31] Sentence Pattern Identification #1

DIRECTIONS: Identify the proper sentence pattern. Use S-V, S-V-O and so forth.

1. English is a Germanic language.
2. The girls danced well.
3. Our new neighbors seemed friendly.
4. Her pies looked delicious.
5. The police questioned the suspect for eight hours.
6. Her arm felt good in a sling.
7. Jane sings beautifully.
8. Bill developed an infection in his eye.
9. The wound must have been very painful.
10. Their class president is Tom Jones.
11. A sergeant became the new commander.
12. The sentence on the board was correct.
13. Jan wrote a story for our literary magazine.
14. Unemployment remains a serious problem for those without work.
15. A steak has never smelled better to me.
16. He cultivated his garden every spring.
17. The pear tasted strange.
18. The play began smoothly.
19. The line appeared straight.
20. The material felt smooth to the touch.

21. Often the newspaper only skims the surface of the news.
22. Many news stories compete for attention.
23. The articles rarely go into depth.
24. Even so, many readers give the paper only a glance.
25. Sometimes they only read the headlines.
26. Headlines seldom tell them the necessary facts.
27. Reporters may give their readers important details.
28. The make-up man may eliminate those details.
29. Advertisers send their customers messages in the newspaper.
30. Advertising lends the newspaper financial support.
31. Usually the newspaper gives its advertisers ample space.
32. Some famous newspapers have died in recent decades.
33. Some readers may remember a paper that no longer exists.
34. Those papers gave employment to many journalists.
35. The deaths of those papers may have taught journalists a lesson.
36. Our team was victorious.
37. The flowers smell very good.
38. The boy sent his parents a telegram.
39. Lincoln may have been our greatest president.
40. The fog comes in on little cat feet.
41. The ship was sailing westward.
42. Kenny has grown quite tall.
43. She introduced her father to her friends.
44. The home team scored only one run.
45. The children were running to the corner.
46. Dad brought the charity a dollar.
47. His argument seemed unbeatable.
48. The captain sounded the alarm.
49. We bought a painting from the artist.
50. Her new doll soon became her favorite.

Sentence Pattern Identification #2

DIRECTIONS: Identify the proper sentence pattern. Use S-V, S-V-O and so forth.

1. He gave her some money.
2. John eats tamales.
3. The dog ran away.
4. The bee stung the bear.
5. That's the truth.
6. The apple became rotten.
7. The milk turned sour.
8. Horses are quick.
9. Hercules gave the world a lift.
10. This morning was chilly.
11. The ceiling fell in.
12. Puppies become dogs.
13. Henry left for town yesterday.
14. The policeman caught the thief.
15. No birds sang.

16. I sent him some of the best peaches.
17. The ice remained hard.
18. The ice remained a frozen mass.
19. All teachers give their students some tests.
20. Pete Rose has hit many homers.
21. Bloodhounds smell well.
22. Bloodhounds smell good.
23. The first man on the block to own a race car wrecked.
24. He ran into a parked car on the side of the road.
25. No one actually saw the accident taking place.

Sentence Pattern Identification #3

DIRECTIONS: Identify the proper sentence pattern. Use S-V, S-V-O and so forth.

1. Rats prowl our cities.
2. They have sharp yellow teeth.
3. They eat garbage.
4. They carry disease.
5. They even smell bad.
6. The rat population is huge.
7. Over 100 million rats live in the United States.
8. They bite 14,000 children per year.
9. Rats can be very dangerous.
10. They crawl behind walls in houses.
11. They usually attack after dark.
12. Rats are everywhere.
13. We must fight rats continuously.
14. Poison works fairly well most of the time.
15. Some poison only gives the rats a stomach ache.
16. Other poisons kill them outright.
17. A good poison gives a quick result.
18. Rats originated in Asia.
19. They came to Europe hundreds of years ago.
20. They spread the Black Death in the 14th century.
21. Rats are fast breeders.
22. Females can have five litters a year.
23. Each litter may have eight or ten babies.
24. Rats are a serious menace to mankind.
25. Kill a rat today for the benefit of mankind.

Sentence Pattern Identification #4

DIRECTIONS: Identify the proper sentence pattern. Use S-V, S-V-O and so forth.

1. A computer has many uses.
2. Some computers are very expensive.
3. The home computer is usually a microcomputer.
4. The C-64 is a good example of a once popular micro.
5. The C-64 was capable of doing many tasks.
6. It could do many mathematical calculations quickly.
7. It also had word processing capabilities.
8. Of course, the software made the difference.
9. A few computers had some programs built into ROM.
10. Those computers did not sell very well initially.
11. The Adam by Coleco is one such example.
12. Software is becoming increasingly sophisticated.
13. Databases and spreadsheets are quite popular.
14. Games are also high on the list for most people.
15. Some games take lots of thought and strategy.
16. Arcade games require quick reactions.
17. Both types are fun to play at times.
18. Some games give you a real test of your abilities.
19. Adventure games ask questions of the user.
20. Simulations set up situations often based on facts.
21. Educational programming is a large part of the market also.
22. Some educational software is really just games.
23. Much educational software drills the student about facts.
24. Newer programs try to be interactive with the user.
25. Soon a whole new generation of software will arrive.

Sentence Pattern Identification #5

DIRECTIONS: Identify the proper sentence pattern. Use S-V, S-V-O and so forth.

1. At that time the Midians prevailed against Israel.
2. The Israelites lived in caves and strongholds.
3. The Lord caused this for seven years.
4. The Midianites and Amalakites were a multitude.
5. They and their camels were uncountable.
6. They came to destroy the land of Israel.
7. The people of Israel cried out to God for help.
8. God sent them a prophet instead of deliverance.
9. The prophet reminded the Israelites that they had disobeyed.
10. That message was not too popular with the Israelites.
11. Then the Lord came to Gideon in the guise of an angel.
12. Gideon was threshing wheat in the winepress.
13. He was hiding from his enemies.
14. God talked to Gideon about the situation.
15. Gideon could not understand their poor straits.
16. God then told Gideon about His plans to use Gideon.
17. Gideon was flabbergasted by the thought.
18. After some discussion it became clear to Gideon.
19. God had chosen him to free Israel.
20. Gideon requested some signs from God to be sure.
21. The signs were really miracles of a sort.
22. His father's altar was blasphemous to God.
23. It was an altar to Baal, a false god of humanism.
24. Gideon tore down the altar of Baal that night.
25. It was an act of faith on Gideon's part.

Sentence Pattern Identification #6

DIRECTIONS: Identify the proper sentence pattern. Use S-V, S-V-O and so forth.

1. Sammy led the league in home runs.
2. The roof caved in.
3. The sun was already hot.
4. Mother scrambled the eggs.
5. Birds travel great distances.
6. Arthur gave Hilda a birthday kiss.
7. That woman is my aunt.
8. The stream trickled downhill.
9. A stitch in time saves nine.
10. Robert Frost was a famous poet.
11. Magellan explored the South Pacific.
12. The guide found a sheltered spot along the trail.
13. The train raced through the long divide.
14. The hikers were ravenously hungry.
15. Howard bought a new home for his family.
16. The operator read Jim the telegram.

17. The workman looks tired.
18. The polite young man in the blue suit is my cousin.
19. The winner was a Spanish girl from Hermosillo.
20. The gentle call of the bird floated away on the breeze.
21. We papered the wall with a large map of Indonesia.
22. Alice visited Wonderland.
23. The crafty fox led the chase up a rocky gulch on Mt. Baldy.
24. Mom bought a vacuum with eight attachments.
25. The girls with bare feet were all surfers.
26. The actress appeared on stage.
27. The eager tourist began to investigate the cataracts.
28. A new hydroelectric plant in Nevada broke down yesterday.
29. George Washington is the father of our country.
30. Elsa has lost her new sweater.
31. The expert gambler never cut the deck fairly.
32. The ice was remaining hard until late afternoon.
33. My best friend just graduated from college.
34. The boys threw the dog a bone.
35. I will go down to the sea again.
36. The new game soon wore our patience down.
37. All words must be morphemes.
38. They dressed in a hurry for the game.
39. Maude mailed the letters to her parents.
40. She causes her friends pain.
41. My corn might grow tall this year.
42. The teacher divided the class into five groups.
43. The young boys told the scoutmaster the truth.
44. We wish you a Merry Christmas.
45. The horses are growing old.
46. The boys with the suits were all young executives.
47. Their children have been running from the dog.
48. He issued new stamps to us for the holiday.
49. Advertisers frequently avoid long words.
50. The old fellow in the car is a friend of mine from school.

[39] Transformation Exercise #1

DIRECTIONS: Transform the following sentences.

YES/NO
1. He will be home by five o'clock.
2. That man was my friend.
3. He has been reading his Bible for many years.
4. We honored the actors with a standing ovation.
5. A good dog barks at strangers.

THERE + BE
6. A boy is working in the barn.
7. Many men are on the fire line.
8. A big horse was prancing around the table.
9. Twenty-three hunters were near Bald Mountain at one time.

10. My friend from school is in Sunday School.
PASSIVE
11. The fisherman landed a barracuda.
12. An Abenaki Indian threw the hatchet with consummate skill.
13. The navigator was turning the plane toward home.
14. Herman had brought his mother a dozen roses.
15. The rifleman had been firing his gun for a long time.
WRITE THE BASE FORMS
16. There are some pigs in the cornfield.
17. Did the farmer know it?
18. They were found in the corn by the hired man.
19. Do the pigs get out often?
20. There are lots of holes in the fence.
21. A large hole was made by the old boar.
22. Was the farmer mad?
23. Will he repair the fence?
24. The fence has been repaired many times.
25. The wire may be bought by the farmer.

Transformation Exercise #2

DIRECTIONS: Write the base forms of the transformations below.

1. The fort had been raided by Apaches.
2. The horses were being eaten by the wolves.
3. Is that too difficult to understand?
4. The original attack was signaled by Yellow Belly himself.
5. Have you faced red savages at dawn?
6. Does this story give you chills?
7. Two soldiers were scalped by Yellow Belly personally.
8. One Indian was trampled by a horse.
9. Guns were used by the soldiers.
10. Primitive weapons were employed by the Indians.
11. Was it a bloodbath?
12. The Indians could have been beaten.
13. One soldier was struck by a flaming arrow.
14. Did he catch on fire?
15. His hair was burned by the flames.
16. One soldier's scalp was severed at the ear by a single blow.
17. Do you believe such a tale?
18. Are you wondering about this exercise?
19. The pony soldiers were dealt a defeat by the Indians.
20. The fort was totally destroyed.
21. There are lots of stories about the cavalry and the Indians.
22. Oh-oh, there is Yellow Belly right behind you.

PASSIVE TRANSFORMATIONS

DIRECTIONS: Change each sentence into a passive construction.

1. The chauffer drove the car.
2. The blow had broken his nose.
3. The wind was blowing the leaves.
4. The best students were using a notebook.
5. A hurricane destroyed the town.
6. The conductor leads the orchestra.
7. A severe storm set back the arrival of the Boston bus.
8. The CFR is a little know group of powerful people.
9. Nelson Rockefeller once headed the organization.
10. The waiter is bringing Tom a menu.
11. Millions of people have seen a Shakespearean play.
12. A special crew may repair the storm damage.
13. I have seen her before.
14. Something interrupted his sleep.
15. Gethron was eating part of the dragon.
16. Good students do their exercises punctually.
17. The king threw out the servant.
18. The teacher gave the boys a workout.
19. The patients were receiving many flowers.
20. That dog should be catching the scent pretty soon.
21. That fellow can eat nine pies at one sitting.
22. One man is fighting a group.
23. One man is watching the races.
24. A Christian should not miss an opportunity to do good.
25. My dog has chased lots of coons.

[52] RP #1

DIRECTIONS: For each set of sentences below make an Rp of S; place in C.

1.	S: The apple was rotten.	C: He ate an apple.
2.	S: His mother was a nurse.	C: The boy ate an apple.
3.	S: It looked odd.	C: I bought a picture.
4.	S: I bought a picture.	C: It looked odd.
5.	S: He is a hero.	C: John shot the bear.
6.	S: Cars use gasoline.	C: Some cars are speedy.
7.	S: The man owns a black dog.	C: The old fellow is a crank.
8.	S: The flower was wilted.	C: He gave the girl a flower.
9.	S: He gave her a flower.	C: John was a good friend.
10.	S: He gave her a flower.	C: The flower was wilted.
11.	S: He gave his girl a flower.	C: She was happy.

Rp #2

DIRECTIONS: For each set of sentences below make an Rp of S; place in C.

1. S: The man usually brings his laundry.   C: The man eats turnips.
2. S: She was his fiance.   C: He gave the girl a diamond ring.
3. S: Malcom was a dirty rat.   C: Malcom liked to play mean tricks on people.
4. S: John went to church with her.   C: I knew the girl.
5. S: His gun was a 16 gauge.   C: Orrin won the shooting contest.

For the following, make Rp's of all the S sentences and place them into the C sentence. You will have only one final sentence for your answer.

6. S: His arm was sore.
   S: The ball was flat.   C: The man threw the ball.
7. S: I like to fish for Bass.
   S: They are a fresh-water variety.   C: Bass are a good sport fish.
8. S: The boulder came crashing down the mountain.
   S: The boulder fell through the roof.
   S: The roof was well-built.   C: The boulder weighed four tons.
9. S: The giant's name was Thorin.
   S: The oxen were stuffed with apples.
   S: Each water barrel held 80 gallons.   C: The giant ate seven oxen and drank
   S: Dinner was held at five o'clock.   three water barrels for dinner.

Rp #3

DIRECTIONS: For the set of sentences below follow each individual set of instructions.

A. Harry has a nice cabin.   B. The cabin is by Folsom Lake.
C. The cabin is made of redwood.   D. Redwood is resistant to rot.
E. Susan visits Harry in the summer.   F. Susan often enjoys Harry's hospitality.
G. Her friendship is highly valued.

1. Rp of A; place in B
2. Rp of A; place in C
3. Rp of A; place in E
4. Rp of B; place in A
5. Rp of B; place in C
6. Rp of C; place in A
7. Rp of C; place in B
8. Rp of C; place in D
9. Rp of D; place in C
10. Rp of E; place in A
11. Rp of F; place in A
12. Rp of G, Rp of A; place in E
13. Rp of D, Rp of C; place in A
14. Rp of G; place in F
15. Rp of E; place in F

Rp #4

DIRECTIONS: For the set of sentences below follow each individual set of instructions.

A. Kingsley bought a boat.
B. The boat was quite fast.
C. The boat was coated with fiberglass.
D. Fiberglass protects the hull.
E. Alice likes to fish with Kingsley.
F. Alice prefers Kingsley's companionship.
G. Her interests usually involve him.

1. Rp of A; place in B
2. Rp of A; place in C
3. Rp of A; place in E
4. Rp of B; place in A
5. Rp of B; place in C
6. Rp of C; place in A
7. Rp of C; place in B
8. Rp of C; place in D
9. Rp of D; place in C
10. Rp of E; place in A
11. Rp of F; place in A
12. Rp of G, Rp of A; place in E
13. Rp of D, Rp of C; place in A
14. Rp of G; place in F
15. Rp of E; place in F

Rp #5

DIRECTIONS: For the set of sentences below follow each individual set of instructions.

A. Manfred shot a deer.
B. The deer dropped within a few feet.
C. The deer had a nice set of horns.
D. The horns had five points on each side.
E. A local sports club gave a prize to Manfred.
F. The club appreciated Manfred's skill.
G. The club's trophy is a silver arrow.

1. Rp of A; place in B
2. Rp of A; place in C
3. Rp of A; place in E
4. Rp of B; place in A
5. Rp of B; place in C
6. Rp of C; place in A
7. Rp of C; place in B
8. Rp of C; place in D
9. Rp of D; place in C
10. Rp of E; place in A
11. Rp of F; place in A
12. Rp of G, Rp of A; place in E
13. Rp of D, Rp of C; place in A
14. Rp of G; place in F
15. Rp of E; place in F

Rp #6

DIRECTIONS: For the set of sentences below follow each individual set of instructions.

A. Allan ate the taco.
C. The taco had salsa on the top.
E. The waitress brought some water for Allan.
G. His tips were usually a dollar.

B. Beef and beans filled the taco.
D. The salsa was very hot.
F. She liked Allan's tips.

1. Rp of A; place in B
2. Passive of A; Rp of A; place in C
3. Rp of A; place in E
4. Passive of B; Rp of B; place in A
5. Rp of B; place in C
6. Rp of C; place in A
7. Rp of C; place in B
8. Rp of C; place in D
9. Rp of D; place in C
10. Rp of E; place in A
11. Rp of F; place in A
12. Rp of G, Rp of A; place in E
13. Rp of D, Rp of C; place in A
14. Rp of G; place in F
15. Passive of E; Rp of E; place in A

Rp #7

DIRECTIONS: For the sentences below, follow each individual set of instructions.

A. Egbert swallowed a toad.
C. The warts were big and ugly.
E. Egbert bought some anti-wart medicine.
G. His fee was only one dollar.

B. The toad had warts on his back.
D. The toad had horns by his ears.
F. A nice doctor treated Egbert.

1. Rp of A; place in B
2. Passive of A; Rp of A; place in B
3. Rp of A; place in E
4. Passive of F; Rp of F; place in A
5. Rp of B; place in C
6. Rp of C; place in B
7. Rp of G; place in F
8. Rp of D; place in B
9. Rp of B; place in D
10. Rp of E; place in A
11. Rp of F; place in A
12. Rp of G, Rp of F; place in E
13. Rp of B; place in A
14. Rp of C, Rp of B; place in D
15. Passive of E; Rp of E; place in F

Rp #8

DIRECTIONS: For the sentences below, follow each individual set of instructions.

A. Oscar reads his Bible daily.
C. The Bible has a leather cover.
E. Ivan likes to worship with Oscar.
G. Ivan teaches classes at the church.

B. The Bible is an heirloom.
D. The cover protects the pages.
F. Ivan attends Oscar's church.

1. Rp of A; place in B
2. Passive of A; Rp of A; place in C
3. Rp of A; place in E
4. Rp of B; place in A
5. Rp of B; place in C
6. Rp of C; place in A
7. Rp of C; place in B
8. Rp of C; place in D
9. Passive of D; Rp of D; place in C
10. Rp of E; place in A
11. Passive of F; Rp of F; place in A
12. Rp of G, Rp of A; place in E
13. Rp of D, Rp of C; place in A
14. Rp of G; place in F
15. Rp of E; place in F

Rp #9

DIRECTIONS: For the sentences below, follow each individual set of instructions.

A. Elmer eats his steak daily.
C. The steak contains much protein.
E. Nancy likes to eat with Elmer.
G. Nancy especially likes the desserts with those meals.

B. Steak is an expensive meal.
D. The protein builds body cells.
F. Nancy enjoys Elmer's meals.

1. Rp of A; place in B
2. Passive of A; Rp of A; place in C
3. Rp of A; place in E
4. Rp of B; place in A
5. Rp of B; place in C
6. Rp of C; place in A
7. Rp of C; place in B
8. Rp of C; place in D
9. Passive of D; Rp of D; place in C
10. Rp of E; place in A
11. Passive of F; Rp of F; place in A
12. Rp of G, Rp of A; place in E
13. Rp of D, Rp of C; place in A
14. Rp of G; place in F
15. Rp of E; place in F

Rp/Transformation #1

DIRECTIONS: Transform the first ten sentences from active to passive or passive to active. For the last sentences, follow the individual directions.

1. The dog chased the pheasant.
2. The pheasant was being hunted by Jack.
3. Jack suddenly saw the pheasant.
4. Jack fired his gun.
5. Jack shot the pheasant.
6. The pheasant had been crippled by the shot.
7. The dog found the pheasant.
8. The dog began to bite the pheasant.
9. The pheasant was eventually eaten by the dog.
10. Jack beat his dog.

11. Rp of 1; place in 2
12. Passive of 1; Rp of 1; place in 2
13. Rp of 10; place in 9
14. Passive of 10; Rp of 10; place in 9
15. Rp of 7; place in 10
16. Passive of 7; Rp of 7; place in 10

Rp/Transformation #2

DIRECTIONS: Transform the first five sentences from active to passive or passive to active. For the last sentences, follow the individual directions.

1. Albert ate the taco.
2. The taco was made by a Mexican cook.
3. The cook had put hot chilies in the taco.
4. The taco burned Albert's mouth.
5. The cook did not like Albert.

6. Rp of 1; place in 5
7. Passive of 1; Rp of 1; place in 2
8. Rp of 4; place in 5
9. Rp of 2; place in 1
10. Rp of 3; place in 4
11. Passive of 3; Rp of 3; place in 4
12. Rp of 3 (cook); place in 2
13. Rp of 3; place in 1
14. Passive of 5; Rp of 5; place in 1
15. Rp of 5; place in 1

Rp/Transformation #3

DIRECTIONS: For the sentences below, follow each individual set of instructions.

A. Zane was following a cold trail.
C. The outlaw was big and ugly.
E. Orick had robbed Zane's hardware store.
G. Orick feared Zane.

B. Zane was looking for an outlaw.
D. The outlaw's name was Orick.
F. Zane had no experience with outlaws.
H. Zane loved a tough fight.

1. Passive of A
2. Passive of E
3. Passive of F
4. Passive of H
5. Rp of A; place in B
6. Rp of D; place in C
7. Rp of E; place in H
8. Rp of G; place in A
9. Rp of B; place in C
10. Passive of B; Rp of B; place in C
11. Passive of G; Rp of G; place in H
12. Passive of G, Rp of G; place in D
13. Rp of C; Rp of H; place in B
14. Rp of B, Rp of C; place in A
15. Rp of G; Rp of H; place in F

Rp/Transformation #4

DIRECTIONS: For the sentences below, follow each individual set of instructions.

A. Omar was reading a telephone book.
C. The girl was very wealthy.
E. Linda had captured Omar's imagination.
G. Linda hardly knew Omar.

B. Omar was looking for a girl.
D. The girl's name was Linda.
F. Omar had few dealings with girls.
H. Omar wanted a female friend.

1. Passive of A
2. Passive of E
3. Passive of F
4. Passive of H
5. Rp of A; place in B
6. Rp of D; place in C
7. Rp of E; place in H
8. Rp of G; place in A
9. Rp of B; place in C
10. Passive of B; Rp of B; place in C
11. Passive of G; Rp of G; place in H
12. Passive of G, Rp of G; place in D
13. Rp of C; Rp of H; place in B
14. Rp of B, Rp of C; place in A
15. Rp of G; Rp of H; place in F

[75] MODIFIER - CONNECTIVE #1

A. Oscar hunts a lot with a dog.   B. His dog is a retriever.
C. The dog's name is Frank Buck.   D. Frank retrieves birds for Oscar.
E. Frank brings them back alive.

1. Coor A & B.
2. Coor C & D.
3. Sub B; place behind A.
4. Sub E; place behind C.
5. Sub A; place before B.
6. Rp of C; place in A.
7 & 8. Rp of B; place in A. (two answers)
9 & 10. Rp of E; place in D. (two answers)
11 & 12. Rp of A; place in D. (two answers)
13 & 14. Rp of E; place in B. (two answers)
15. Passive of E; Rp of E; place in D. (use *birds* as related item)

MODIFIER - CONNECTIVE #2

A. The door was made of oak.
B. Harry closed the door.
C. Harry was a Marine.

1. Coor A & B.
2. Coor B & C.
3. Coor A & C.
4. Sub B; place behind A.
5. Sub B; place before C.
6. Rp of A; place in B.
7. Rp of C; place in B.
8. Rp of B; place in A.
9 & 10. Rp of B; place in C. (two answers)
11. Passive of B; Rp of B; place in A.
12. Appositive of C; place in B.
13. Single word participle of B; place in A.
14. Participle phrase of B; place in A.
15. One word modifier of A; place in B.

MODIFIER - CONNECTIVE #3

A. We painted the shutters.
B. The shutters were on the house.
C. The shutters had four hinges.

1. Coor A & B.
2. Coor B & C.
3. Coor A & C.
4. Sub A; place before B.
5. Sub B; place behind C.
6. Rp of A; place in B.
7. Rp of B; place in A.
8. Rp of C; place in A.
9. Rp of B; place in C.
10. Rp of B & C; place in A.
11. Passive of A; Rp of A; place in C.
12. One word modifier of B; place in A.
13. One word participle of A; place in B.
14. Participle phrase of A; place in C.
15. One word modifier of C; place in A.

MODIFIER - CONNECTIVE #4

A. The stallion threw the cowboy.
B. The cowboy worked for the Bar-X Ranch.
C. The cowboy's name was Slim.
D. The stallion was a fighter.

1. Coor A & B.
2. Coor B & C.
3. Use c/a between A & D.
4. Sub A; place before B.
5. Sub C; place behind B.
6. Rp of A; place in B.
7. Rp of B; place in A.
8. Rp of C; place in B.
9. Rp of D; place in A.
10. Rp of A & D; place in B.
11. Passive of A; Rp of A; place in B.
12. Appositive of C; place in B.
13. One word participle of A; place in B.
14. Participle phrase of A; place in B.
15. Appositive of D; place in A.

MODIFIER - CONNECTIVE #5

A. Paul preached in Rome.
B. Rome was the center of the empire.
C. Rome was very powerful.
D. God protected Paul.

1. Coor A & D.
2. Coor B & C.
3. Use c/a between A & D.
4. Sub A; place before B.
5. Sub C; place behind A.
6. Rp of A; place in B.
7. Rp of B; place in A.
8. Rp of C; place in B.
9. Rp of A; place in D.
10. Rp of D & B, place in A.
11. Passive of D; Rp of D; place in A.
12. Rp of A & C place in D.
13. One word modifier of C; place in A.
14. Participle phrase of D; place in A.
15. Appos of B; place in C.

MODIFIER - CONNECTIVE #6

A. Homer is a cat.
C. The milk is kept cool.
E. Homer is lazy.

B. Homer likes milk.
D. Arthur delivers the milk.
F. He is a Persian.

1. Coor A & B.
2. Coor E & F.
3. Use c/a between B & C.
4. Sub B; place behind A.
5. Sub F; place behind E.
6. Sub E; place before F.
7. Rp of B; place in A.
8. Rp of C; place in B.
9. Rp of D; place in C.
10. Rp of B & C; place in D.
11. Passive of D; Rp of D; place in B.
12. Appos of F; place in E.
13. Appos of A; place in B.
14. One word modifier of C; place in B.
15. One word modifier of E; place in A.

MODIFIER - CONNECTIVE #7

A. The man is a mason.
C. The fireplaces keep houses warm.
E. Home owners often call on the man.

B. The man builds fireplaces.
D. The man's house has a large fireplace.

1. Coor A & B.
2. Coor B & C.
3. Use c/a between A & D.
4. Sub C; place before B.
5. Sub C; place behind D.
6. Sub A; place before D.
7. Rp of D; place in A.
8. Rp of A; place in B.
9. Rp of B; place in C.
10. Rp of B & C; place in E.
11. Passive of B; Rp of B; place in C.
12. Rp of E; place in B.
13. Appos of A; place in B.
14. Participle phrase of B; place in C.
15. One word modifier of C; place in D.

MODIFIER - CONNECTIVE #8

A. The hunter was stalking the bear.
C. The hunter followed the bear's tracks.
E. The bear bit the hunter.

B. The bear was a grizzly.
D. The hunter disappeared behind a tree.

1. Coor A & B.
2. Use c/a between C & D.
3. Sub D; place before E.
4. Rp of A; place in B.
5. Rp of E; place in D.
6. Rp of D; place in A.
7. Rp of C; place in B.
8. Passive of C; Rp of C; place in B.
9. Passive of E; Rp of E; place in D.
10. Appos of B; place in E.
11. One word participle of A; place in D.
12. Participle phrase of A; place in C.
13. Participle phrase of E; place in C.
14. One word modifier of B; place in A.
15. One word modifier of A; place in E.

MODIFIER - CONNECTIVE #9

DIRECTIONS: Find the number of the sentence that fits the instruction and mark it down. If no sentence provided fits the instruction, write NONE by the number and write out the sentence that fits.

A. The drifter was floating the river.
B. The river was the Rogue.
C. The river was swift.
D. The drifter followed the river's currents.
E. The river fooled the drifter.
F. The drifter went into the rocks.

1. Coor B & C.
2. Use c/a between E & F.
3. Sub E; place before F.
4. Sub D; place behind F.
5. Sub C; place before D.
6. Sub C; place behind A.
7. Rp of C; place in A.
8. Rp of E; place in F.
9. Rp of D; place in C.
10. Rp of A; place in D.
11. Rp of F & B; place in A.
12. Passive of A; Rp of A; place in B.
13. Passive of E; Rp of E; place in F.
14. Appositive of B; place in C.
15. One word participle of A; place in E.
16. Participial phrase of A; place in F.
17. Participial phrase of E; place in D.
18. One word participle of E; place in F.
19. One word modifier of B; place in E.
20. One word modifier of C; place in B.

1. The drifter was floating the Rogue River.
2. The drifter was floating the swift river.
3. The drifter was floating the river because it was swift.
4. The drifter was floating the river, and it fooled him.
5. The drifter was floating the river which was the Rogue.
6. The drifter was floating the river which was swift.
7. The drifter who the river fooled was floating the river.
8. The drifter who the river fooled went into the rocks.
9. The drifter whom the river fooled followed the river's current.
10. The drifter whom the river fooled went into the rocks.
11. The drifter who was floating the river followed the river's current.
12. The drifter who followed the river's current was floating the river.
13. The drifter who went into the rocks was floating the river.
14. The drifter who was fooled by the river went into the rocks.
15. The drifter floating the river followed the river's current.
16. The drifter floating the river went into the rocks.
17. The floating drifter followed the river's current.
18. The floating drifter went into the rocks.
19. The Rogue River was swift.
20. The river was the Rogue, and it was swift.
21. The river was swift, yet the drifter followed its current.
22. Since the river was swift, the drifter followed its current.
23. The river was swift; therefore, the drifter followed its current.
24. The river was swift although the drifter followed its current.
25. The river fooled the drifter, and he went into the rocks.
26. The drifter fooled by the river went into the rocks.
27. The drifter was fooled by river so he went into the rocks.
28. When the drifter went into the rocks, he followed the river's current.
29. The river that fooled the drifter was the Rogue.

MODIFIER - CONNECTIVE #10

A. The man is a fireman.
C. The truck is spotless.
E. The man is lying on his bunk.

B. The man appreciates the truck.
D. The chief drives the truck.
F. The local children all know the man.

1. Rp of A; place in B.
2. Rp of F; place in B.
3. Rp of D; place in C.
4. Rp of C; place in D.
5. Part phrase of E; place in B.
6. -en part phrase of D; place in C.
7. Passive of F; Rp of F; place in E.
8. Appos of A; place in E.
9. Single -en part of B; place in C.
10. Single word modifier of C; place in B.

MODIFIER - CONNECTIVE #11

A. The girl is an actress.
C. The scene is comical.
E. The girl is playing a piano.

B. The girl enjoys this scene.
D. A male star crashes the scene.
F. The fans really like the actress.

1. Rp of A; place in B.
2. Rp of F; place in B.
3. Rp of D; place in C.
4. Rp of C; place in D.
5. Part phrase of E; place in B.
6. -en part phrase of D; place in C.
7. Passive of F; Rp of F; place in E.
8. Appos of A; place in E.
9. Single word -en part of B; place in C.
10. Single word modifier of C; place in B.
11. Passive of B; Rp of B; place in D.
12. Rp of A; Rp of C; place in B.
13. Rp of A; Rp of F; place in E.
14. Single word -en participle of D; place in B.
15. Single word -en participle of F; place in A.

PART 1: follow each individual set of directions; spell & punctuate properly.

Transform these four sentences to the passive.

1. The man hit the ball.
2. The dog is chasing the truck.
3. The subject usually precedes the object.
4. They may have eaten everything.

A) The man was a knight.   B) The man was Don Quixote.

5. Appos of B; place in A.
6. Rel of A; place in B.

A) The girls like Don Juan.   B) Don Juan is a lover.

7. Rp of A; place in B.
8. Appos. of B; place in A.
9. -EN part. phrase of A; place in B

A) Arthur commanded the army.   B) Mordred defeated the army at Maldon.

10. Rp of B; place in A.
11. -EN part. phrase of A; place in B.
12. Single word -EN part. of B; place in A.

A) Gawain heard the priest.   B) The priest was telling a story.

13. Part. phrase of B; place in A.
14. Part. phrase of A; place in B.
15. Rp of B; place in A.

PART 2: Identify the following structures with the proper abbreviation; CAUTION: more than one item per blank may occur; if none of the structures occur, write NONE in the blank.
appos = appositive   ger = gerund   rel = relative clause   part = participle   pass = passive   inf = infinitive

16. The man who threw the broken lance rode a black charger.
17. The charger was large and quick to respond to commands on the field.
18. The horse was capable of shifting its position on the field at any moment.
19. The man riding the charger was an earl, a man of great honor.
20. He rode that same black charger into battle many times before his eventual death in combat.
21. His last request before dying was to have his charger buried with him.
22. Both of them were buried in one grave by some of their loyal followers.
23. It was a bleak day for those who loved the earl.
24. It is difficult for some to understand such actions of loving devotion.
25. Such a story strikes at the root of human emotions, the spirit of man.

MODIFIER - CONNECTIVE #13

PART 1: follow each individual set of directions; spell & punctuate properly.

Transform these four sentences to the passive.

1. The boy ate the apple.
2. The spider is catching the bug.
3. A direct object never follows a linking verb.
4. We must have taken all the food.

A) The lady was a nurse.   B) The lady was Florence Nightengale.

5. Appos of B; place in A.
6. Rel of A; place in B.

A) The dogs chase Taffy.   B) Taffy is a thief.

7. Rp of A; place in B.
8. Appos. of B; place in A.
9. -EN part. phrase of A; place in B.

A) Chin Tsu worked the mine.   B) An Irishman found the mine.

10. Rp of B; place in A.
11. -EN part. phrase of A; place in B.
12. Single word -EN part. of B; place in A.

A) The sniper spotted an enemy.   B) The enemy was loading his gun.

13. Part. phrase of B; place in A.
14. Part. phrase of A; place in B.
15. Rp of B; place in A.

PART 2: Identify the following structures by writing the proper abbreviation; CAUTION: more than one item per senctence may occur; if none of the structures occur, write NONE for the sentence.

appos - appositive   ger - gerund   rel - relative clause   part - participle   pass - passive   inf - infinitive

16. A loud cry was heard over the brow of the hill which was just off to the left.
17. The leader of the group was quick to react, and he was very deliberate.
18. The leader, a chief, motioned to one of his trusted men.
19. A tall brave carrying a short bow moved with silence to the old chief.
20. They spoke in almost inaudible tones, and then the brave broke into a trot toward the rear.
21. The chief watched him briefly before turning to the others who were still waiting alertly.
22. Again the chief motioned, and they fell into step quietly behind him as he moved out.
23. They began veering to the left around the hill which waited in silence.
24. Suddenly a piercing cry reached their now very alert and suspicious ears.
25. Something was wrong, but they trusted their chief, a man of many battles.

GRAMMAR TERMS

Grammar, like so many other things in life, is a matter of terminology. If you want to master grammar, you will need to know the language of grammar. It is the same with math, medicine, music, finance, and so forth. Since the table of contents is almost as good as an index in itself, I have determined that a list of terms would be more helpful. The terms are roughly alphabetical. That means under certain terms you will find other related terms.

ADJECTIVE (A): Its function is to describe or modify a noun. Adjectives have three forms of degree: positive (simple 1), comparative (*-ER* 2), and superlative (*-EST* 3+).

ADJECTIVE SUBJECT COMPLEMENT (Asc): complements the subject; it describes the subject but is found in the predicate.

ADVERB (B): Adverbs generally modify a verb; they give additional information about the verb according to TIME (when), MANNER (how), or PLACE (where).

AGREEMENT: This is between the subject and the verb; their respective forms must agree with one another. For instance, ONE BOY RUNS, but MANY BOYS RUN.

ANTECEDENT: the word (noun) for which the pronoun stands. In order, it comes before its substitute.

APPOSITIVE (APPOS): a noun or a pronoun acting as a noun that follows another noun to explain or rename it.

BASEWORD: Also **HEADWORD**, it is the word which serves as the focus for other words in a group.

CLUSTER: a group of words all centering around a baseword.

CONJUNCTIONS: Connectors, words used to connect two ideas together. This text identifies three types of conjunctions used in the addition method of sentence combining.

    CONJUNCTIVE ADVERB (c/a): a weak connector requiring punctuation on both sides; commom c/a's are *however, nevertheless, therefore, hence.*

    COORDINATING CONJUNCTION (c/c): connectors of any two equal grammatical units; the FANBOYS: *for, and, nor, but, or, yet, so.*

    SUBORDINATING CONJUNCTION (sub): a word that joins two thoughts together but makes one dependent on the other; common subs are *if, when, although, as, because*

DEPENDENT CLAUSE: a clause that cannot stand by itself; it is not a complete sentence.

GERUND: see VERBAL.

INDEPENDENT CLAUSE (I): complete sentence, a grammatical unit consisting of subject and predicate that makes complete sense in itself. See SENTENCE.

INDIRECT OBJECT (IO): the receiver of the direct object.

INFINITIVE: see VERBAL.

INTENSIFIERS: words that limit the range of an adjective or an adverb. They always occur with an adjective or an adverb, never alone. Some grammars label intensifiers as adverbs. The most common intensifier is *very*.

MODIFY: to limit or qualify, usually associated with adjectives and adverbs.

NOUN (N): In English this type of word is used to give names to persons, places, and things. An easy way to remember a noun is to think of it as a namer.

> **COMMON NOUN:** refers to any one of a class or group of beings or lifeless things or even the collection itself; also it can refer to a quality, action, condition, or general idea.

> **PLURAL:** the form of a noun that represents two or more.

> **PROPER NOUNS:** refer to a specific or particular individual or thing. They are always capitalized.

> **SINGULAR:** the form of a noun representing one item.

NOUN BASEWORD (Nbw): the main noun in a cluster of modifiers grouped around it.

NOUN CLUSTER (Ncl): the group of words that form around a noun baseword (Nbw).

NOUN MARKER (NM): a word that marks a noun; the three most common NM's are *a, an,* and *the*.

NOUN SUBJECT COMPLEMENT (Nsc): complements the subject, it is a second name for the subject but is found in the predicate.

OBJECT (O): also **DIRECT OBJECT**, the receiver of the action (direct object).

OBJECT PREPOSITION (OP): the last word in a prepositional phrase; it is almost always a noun.

PARALLELISM: a concept that is linked to using grammatical constructions in series. The parallelism rule simply states that the various parts of the series must all have the same construction.

PARTICIPLE: see VERBAL.

PASSIVE: said of verbs and sentences, it changes the word order in sentences. See TRANSFORMATIONS.

PREPOSITION (P): a function word or a structure word. It is used to glue other words together, usually two nouns. The preposition will show either a time or a space relationship. Most prepositions show a space relationship.

PREPOSITIONAL PHRASE (Pp): a group of words beginning with a preposition and ending with its object The formula is P + ... OP with the ... representing anything in between.

PRONOUNS For this text, it is both the class of words that take the place of nouns, in which case we will simply call them nouns, and those that act as NM's, also called pronominals or pronominal adjectives by some.

>   **CASE:** shown by personal pronouns, there are three different cases, nominative or subject case, accusative or object case, possessive or genitive case.

>   **GENDER:** shown by personal pronouns, there are three genders: masculine, feminine, and neuter.

>   **PERSON:** shown by personal pronouns, there are three persons: 1st person speaks, 2nd person is spoken to, and 3rd person is spoken about.

RELATIVE (R): The basic relatives are *who, whom, whose, which, that* (+ *whoever, whomever*). These words relate a clause to another noun in the sentence, usually previous to the clause.

> **RELATIVE PATTERN (Rp):** Also **RELATIVE CLAUSE,** a clause, usually beginning with a relative, which modifies a noun or once in a while stands for a noun.

SENTENCE: A basic sentence is a sentence that is simple, declarative, and in the active voice.

>   **PREDICATE:** comes second and is the telling part. It always contains a verb.

>   **SUBJECT:** This is the naming part of the sentence. It comes first and contains either a noun or a word or phrase functioning as a noun.

>>   **SIMPLE SUBJECT:** It is the noun baseword of the cluster serving as subject in a sentence.

SENTENCE COMBINING: either putting two or more sentences into one or ideas from other sentences into a new sentence.

>   **ADDITION:** In this method two sentences are combined by simply adding the one sentence to the other.

>   **EMBEDDING:** In this method some part of the source sentence is extracted and placed or embedded into the consumer sentence.

SIBILANT: letters making a hissing sound (*s, sh, ch, x, z*)

SUFFIX: a syllable added to the end of a word.

>   **INFLECTIONAL:** a change of form that alters meaning but not word type; shows some grammatical relationship: number, case, degree, etc.

>   **DERIVATIONAL:** a change of form that alters both the meaning and the word type.

SYNTAX: word order, important in determining the relationships of words in English.

TEST FRAME: a sentence with a blank in it used to test words to see if they are a particular type of word. This test is most useful in eliminating word classes.

TRANSFORMATIONS: sentences that have had their normal word order adjusted. Three types of common transformations exist: yes/no questions, *there + be* constructions, and passives.

VERB (V): the telling words; they generally tell what the subject is doing except for linking verbs.

    ACTIVE VERBS: all verbs that are not linking; they show action of some sort.

    AUXILIARY VERB: a verb which helps the main verb; generally modals and forms of *have* and *be*.

    INTRANSITIVE VERB: a verb which does NOT carry action across to an object.

    IRREGULAR VERB: a verb that doesn't form its past forms regularly.

    LINKING VERB (LV): also called state of being verb; there are only 12: *be, become, remain, look, appear, taste, sound, smell, feel, act, grow, seem.*

    MODALS: nine auxiliary verbs that show probability: *can, could, shall, should, will, would, may, might, must.*

    REGULAR VERB: a verb which uses *-ED* for its past forms.

    VERB CLUSTER (Vcl): It is formed around a verb baseword (Vbw); this cluster always follows a very rigid order. The syntax formula is MODAL (+ simple) HAVE (+ en) BE (+ ing) Vbw.

    TRANSITIVE VERB: a verb which carries the action across from the subject to an object.

    VERB BASEWORD (Vbw): the main verb in a cluster of verbs and other modifiers.

VERBAL: a verb which retains some qualities of a verb but does the job of an adjective or a noun. It modifies or acts as a noun substitute. The three types are participles, gerunds, and infinitives.

    GERUND: an *-ING* form of a verb which substitutes for a noun.

    INFINITIVE a *TO* + verb combination which either 1) substitutes for a noun or 2) modifies some part of the sentence.

    PARTICIPLE: an *-ING* or *-EN* form of a verb used as a modifier.

From Heart to Page
Putting Ideas to Paper with Helps

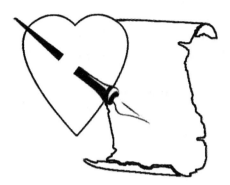

This is a booklet about journaling for young writers. It is designed for grades 4-8 but would be good for any reluctant writer. The book contains topic starters for 180 days. It's great for reluctant writers, young writers, any writer who needs a prompt to get them writing. This easy to use guide helps children move words.

♥ "Michelle Van Loon...makes it easy by suggesting writing prompts for each day. The prompts...are good for all ages and are wide ranging; they deal with events, experiences, observations, feelings, spiritual issues and more. Children who write every day will undoubtedly improve their skills..."
-**Cathy Duffy**, *Christian Home Educators Curriculum Manual*

♥ "It's amazing how many kinds of things there are to write about if you just sit down and think about it. But of course busy homeschooling moms usually don't have that kind of time. I think your booklet provides a real service for people."
-**Jan Burton**, *Editor, Scripture Press*

♥ "It's wonderful! So many ideas...attractively designed, too."
-**Neta Jackson**, *co-author, Trailblazer Books series*

Writing to Change the World
How to Style Your Writing for Publication

Look what you get in this book!

☞ what kind of words to use that grab a reader
☞ how to set up & write various types of articles
☞ tips on plot, character, & details in a short story
☞ what to say in book reviews & who wants them
☞ how to write various kinds of poetry
☞ sample of a query letter and how to write one
☞ exercises to help you practice what you learn
☞ a grade log for you and your teacher
☞ written for teens but profitable for adults

STUDENT: "This book made writing sound so easy. It made me think about becoming a writer. The book made writing sound fun." Ethan Hendricks, 13

HOMESCHOOLING MOM: "As a working and homeschooling mother of five, the self-teach format of *Writing to Change the World* was just what I had

been looking for. My eighth and tenth grade sons enjoyed their creative writing lessons more than they ever have before." - Anita Kimball

AUTHOR: "Who knew learning about grammar and punctuation could be so much fun? This guide presents the creative and technical challenges of writing in a series of intriguing, easy-to-follow lessons. I wish I'd had this book when I was first learning to write." Deborah Chester, author of *The King Betrayed*

TEACHER: *"Writing to Change the World* inspires creativity with clear explanations, examples and encouragement. It contains the building blocks to take the students from sentences to short stories confidently and provides both teacher and student with concrete ways to evaluate an abstract subject. It made me want to write something!"
Carol Daugherty, English teacher, 20 years

English Fun Stuff

✳ Pretentious Proverbs - a vocabulary exercise that teaches wise sayings.

✳ Wordhai - a game of extracting three letter words in the right order.

✳ Idioms & Metaphors - over a hundred colorful phrases to decipher.

✳ Flexibility Puzzles - word combinations with a new twist.

✳ Odd and Even - a great game of logic that has infinite replays.

✳ Logic Puzzles - a series of great mindbenders that force careful thought

✳ Single Events - many fun things to do with words, prefixes, and suffixes.

This book is designed to teach, to entertain, and to help the student work with the language or elements of it. My own students enjoyed these games and exercises, and they learned and stretched their minds at the same time. Use the activities in this book as rewards, diversions, complements, fillers, or exercises; you can even grade some of them and give regular or extra credit. The main point is to learn and have fun at the same time.

Sound Spelling

Look what you get in this book!

✍ an entirely new and effective way to deal with spelling problems
✍ a lifetime speller, good forever, not just a year or two
✍ an individualized program that solves your spelling problems
✍ all the necessary information to become a good speller
✍ a book based on a reliable, common sense principle
✍ a series of sound/letter patterns which unlock the keys to spelling

Wordsmiths
1355 Ferry Road,
Grants Pass, OR 97526

Visit http://www.jsgrammar.com for current titles, prices, and other information.

Look at what these folks have to say!

"Sound Spelling could easily be called Spelling for Dummies. I highly recommend it." Tammy Ryan, editor of The Homeschool at www.hschool.com

"I highly recommend Sound Spelling, especially for older students who work independently. For younger students, I am confident that the program will be most effective with on-going reinforcement and support from parents." Joan Callaway, Program Director, Be Smart! Tutoring Program, Reading Support Monitor on VegSource Homeschooling Board

"We are happy to recommend it. This was a neat way to learn!" Orilla M. Crider, Director, MATCH, Missouri Association of Teaching Homes

"If you are used to old-fashioned spelling workbooks with lists of words and rules to memorize,...[this] will seem strange at first. But, if you are like so many people for whom the traditional method hasn't worked, setting aside the 'school model' of spelling lessons for a totally new concept that is custom-tailored to your specific needs, will be well worth the effort." D. Keith, Editor of Homefires: The Journal of Homeschooling at www.homefires.com

Jensen's Vocabulary

Your Easy Way to a Great Vocabulary

Look what you get in this book!

☞ constant repetition for long term retention
☞ simple format to follow with great results
☞ four reproducible charts of roots & affixes
☞ a systematic approach to learning vocabulary
☞ over 1000 valuable words from basic roots
☞ practice based on a proven system
☞ daily and weekly reinforcement
☞ Latin and Greek based words become easy
☞ a complete package for individual or classroom
☞ four types of exercises for each set of words
☞ easy to follow pattern of instruction
☞ little or no teacher input after the beginning
☞ easy scoring and test methodologies
☞ extensive word parts list for extra help
☞ not a free lunch but a great meal
☞ better scores on tests like SAT, CAT, etc.
☞ easy accountability for teacher and student
☞ complete answer keys for exercises & tests
☞ increased ability to intelligently guess new words
☞ answers to all exercises included for self-scoring

Learn how prefixes, suffixes and roots combine to make all kinds of words.

Learn how to figure out the spelling of a word by the parts that make it up.

Learn how to think in logical fashion about words and their meanings.

Learn a few roots that give you the keys to hundreds of words.

Develop the single most necessary ingredient of good communication: a good vocabulary.

Increase your ability to read and understand as well as express yourself more concisely with these words.

Look at what these folks have to say!

"The students increased their vocabulary scores on the Iowa Test of Basic Skills by 22 percent across the board. That means that all students increased their scores. I was elated." Tim Moore, classroom teacher

"I have used your vocabulary books for several years. Not only do my children enjoy the books very much, but they are learning and retaining the information." Karen Locklair, Senior Instructor

"*Jensen's Vocabulary* has proved very useful in expanding my vocabulary. By studying the structure and learning the meanings of the root words, my vocabulary has increased significantly." Christine Dawson, 14, homeschooled student

"After using Jensen's Grammar and Vocabulary: Latin I with our 7th grader, his achievement test scores increased 18% in total language and 45% in spelling from his previous scores. Thank you. We love your books." Derlyze Breitner, homeschooling mom

"As a former high school English teacher & a present home schooling mom (4 H.S. kids), I enthusiastically endorse your products." Mary Angel, homeschooling mom

What John Saxon did for math, Frode Jensen does for English.

Wordsmiths
1355 Ferry Road
Grants Pass, OR 97526

Visit http://www.jsgrammar.com for current titles, prices, and other information.

Jensen's Punctuation
A Complete Guide to all your Punctuation Needs

Look what you get in this book!

- ☞ a punctuation rule book with examples
- ☞ constant repetition for long term retention
- ☞ a reproducible card of rules for ready reference
- ☞ a list of key words that reveal certain rules
- ☞ exercises taken from classical literature
- ☞ secrets of compound sentence punctuation
- ☞ how to punctuate long & difficult sentences
- ☞ when to use commas with subordinators
- ☞ five simple rules that help immensely
- ☞ where commas go with a conjunctive adverb
- ☞ how to use commas with the FANBOYS
- ☞ when not to use a comma between clauses
- ☞ how to tell independent from dependent clauses
- ☞ easy formulas that can be applied continuously
- ☞ the one word that signals no comma
- ☞ practice in the use of the comma & semicolon
- ☞ complete answer keys for exercises & tests
- ☞ info on grading and scoring exercises & tests

Learn the five basic rules for compound sentences that solve 75-90% of your punctuation problems.

Learn how to use the punctuation index to help you master all the punctuation rules worth knowing.

Learn the three types of key words and how they signal what type of punctuation is needed, if any.

Learn what kinds of words in what kind of situations need capitals and how to identify them in sentences.

Learn when and when not to use a comma with modifiers occurring in various positions in a sentence.

Learn how to correctly use the semi-colon in the most common situation in which it occurs.

Look at what these folks have to say!

"The lessons are quick and painless, about 5-10 minutes each, and you will find these exercises more interesting than what's usually found in grammar texts since they are examples from real books." Teresa Schultz-Jones, national reviewer

"I appreciate the work that went into writing these punctuation books. You have done a good job. I have really seen improvement in my 9th grader's use of punctuation." Joanne Juren, home schooling mom

"I knew there had to be some concrete rules about when and where to apply various punctuation; however, the only instruction I ever got was to just put a comma where you would take a breath. It is a great relief to know the when, where, and why of punctuation, especially when my children want solid answers." Paula Wilcox, home schooling mom

"I am very thankful for the work you have done in preparing these wonderful teaching tools. They are the best I have found." William J. Puderbaugh, Farsight Education

"As a former high school English teacher & a present home schooling mom (4 H.S. kids), I enthusiastically endorse your products." Mary Angel, home schooling mom

What John Saxon did for math, Frode Jensen does for English.

Wordsmiths
1355 Ferry Road
Grants Pass, OR 97526

Visit http://www.jsgrammar.com for current titles, prices, and other information.

Jensen's Format Writing

How to Write Easily and Well

Look what you get in this book!

- ☞ how to write good paragraphs
- ☞ how to do 5 paragraph essays
- ☞ how to organize major papers
- ☞ the seven sentence outline
- ☞ the principle of condensation
- ☞ secrets of the thesis statement
- ☞ how to introduce a topic
- ☞ how to conclude a topic
- ☞ seven practical formats
- ☞ clear & simple instructions
- ☞ learnable procedures
- ☞ instructive examples
- ☞ analytical grading keys
- ☞ how to use note cards
- ☞ how to organize your writing
- ☞ applications for appendices
- ☞ the use of in-text citations & end notes
- ☞ what transitions are and how to use them
- ☞ how to put together a great resume
- ☞ all about point of view and tense shifts

Learn the secret of cutting your work in half when it comes to writing a paper.

Learn how to order your presentation for its most powerful effect on the reader.

Learn a technique for getting the essence of what you read down on paper for future reference.

Learn how to stack up your ideas so that they flow together in a natural fashion.

Learn the art of transitioning from sentence to sentence and paragraph to paragraph.

Learn all about what and how to document your sources when doing research and writing.

Look what these folks have to say!

"This is probably the most comprehensive tool for teaching expository writing at the lowest price." Cathy Duffy, national reviewer

"My daughter just finished English 101 in college and received the only *A* in the class. She said that no book has been so helpful as *Format Writing*." Sally Beardsley, home schooling mom

"I am very impressed with your book *Format Writing* and have recommended it to my clients for some time." Jo Anne Bennett, educational consultant

"My daughter and I discovered *Format Writing* the last two years of her high school career. She worked through it from cover to cover, and I am more than pleased with end result." Peggy Blanchard, home schooling mom

"As a former high school English teacher & a present home schooling mom (4 H.S. kids), I enthusiastically endorse your products." Mary Angel, home schooling mom

"I developed many of these techniques to help me get through college. They work. I know; I've used them." Frode Jensen, author of the text

What John Saxon did for math, Frode Jensen does for English.

Wordsmiths
1355 Ferry Road
Grants Pass, OR 97526

Visit http://www.jsgrammar.com for current titles, prices, and other information.

A Journey Through Grammar Land

A Systematic, Easy to Learn, Tour of Grammar

A modern *Pilgrim's Progress* type allegory that teaches language skills in an enjoyable fashion.

Join Tank and PG as they travel through Grammar Land. Learn with Tank as he meets and interacts with all sorts of people who instruct him and guide him on his journey.

These books cover the Namers and their Substituters. Students will recognize them as Nouns and Pronouns. Then Tank meets with the Tellers or Verbs. Students will easily pick up on proper syntax of helping verbs in combination and also learn who the Linkers are as well as all about the BE family. Later Tank finds out about Adjectives and Adverbs with a trip through the Descriptive Mountains on to the Central Intelligence Adverbial Agency. Learn how Tank and his friends outmaneuver King Falsifier and the renegades in this book. From there Tank learns about Prepositions and Conjunctions. Tour Prepositional Railway Station with him and then go on to Connecting Junction. Tank then moves on to meet the various types of clauses. You will go with him to visit Thought Trucking Terminal where you will learn about simple sentence patterns and from there move on to Clause Village, home of the complex sentence builders. Finally Tank will go to Verbal International Airport where the participles, gerunds, and infinitives are.

CHECK THIS LIST OF BENEFITS FOR YOU & YOUR STUDENT!

✓ Totally self-contained: story, lessons, tests, answers, & teacher helps.
✓ Constant review for long term learning using spaced repetition.
✓ Full story text in front, a grammar synopsis in the back with exercises.
✓ Innovative structure and design, easy to follow presentation.
✓ Minimal teacher preparation time needed.
✓ Successfully used for both initial teaching and remediation.
✓ 5th-7th grades targeted but appropriate for a wide variety of ages.
✓ Solid teaching and coverage of standard material.
✓ An easy yet enjoyable story that teaches about grammar.

> "The Grammar Land books should be useful for a broad range of home schooling situations since they are so user-friendly." *Cathy Duffy*

Notes from the Smithy...

FREE quarterly electronic newsletter, that's right, yours FREE for the asking.

TWO EASY WAYS TO SIGN UP:

Visit our web site at http://www.jsgrammar.com and follow the prompts.
Email me at frodej@jsgrammar.com and ask to subscribe.

Each issue of "Smithy Notes" contains all original articles on teaching, both practical methods and philosophical overviews. There's news about what's going on with the books and the company, and there's always something fun to do, an exercise or puzzle that you can share with your students.

Wordsmiths
1355 Ferry Road
Grants Pass, OR 97526

Visit http://www.jsgrammar.com for current titles, prices, and other information.